VIOLENCE ON WOMEN

By

Dr. Suruchi Shukla
Dr. Anjna Fellows
Dr. Neelma Kunwar

DPH

DISCOVERY PUBLISHING HOUSE PVT. LTD.
NEW DELHI-110 002

Published by:
Tilak Wasan

DISCOVERY PUBLISHING HOUSE PVT. LTD.
4383/4A, Ansari Road, Darya Ganj
New Delhi-110 002 (India)
Phone : +91-11-23279245, 43596064-65
Fax : +91-11-23253475
E-mail : parul.wasan@gmail.com
discoverypublishinghouse@gmail.com
web : www.discoverypublishinggroup.com

***First Edition:* 2012**

ISBN: 978-93-5056-016-7

Violence on Women

Printed at:
Shree Balaji Art Press
Delhi

Preface

Violence affects the lives of millions of women, worldwide in all socio-economic and educational classes. It cuts across cultural and religious barriers impending the right of women to participate fully in society. The violence may involve physical abuse, sexual assault and threats. Sometimes it's more subtle, like making someone feel worthless, not letting them have any money or not allowing them to leave the home. Domestic violence is not just hitting or fighting or an occasional argument it is an abuse of power. All forms of domestic abuse one purpose to gain and maintain total control over the victim. Abusers use many tactics to exert power over their spouse or partner; dominance, humiliation, isolation, threats, intimidation, denial and blame. The form and characteristics of domestic violence and abuse may vary in other ways. Distinctions need to be made regarding type of violence, motives of perpetrators and the social and cultural context. Violence by a person against their intimate partner is often done as a way for controlling 'their partner', even if this kind of violence is not the most frequent. Other types of intimate partner violence also occur including violence between gay and lesbian couples, and by women against their male partners.

Though the articles and scripts were produced in countries of varying cultural and economic situations, they share a common thread. The media, as major purveyors of society's images, can play a key role in breaking down stereotypes and negative attitude towards women.

Suruchi Shukla
Anjna Fellows
Neelma Kunwar

Preface

Acknowledgements

At the very outset I bow in research to alimighty 'God' for his blessings that provided me great zeal and enthusiasm to complete this study. I wish for his blessing every after in my life ahead. It is golden opportunity and proud privilege to work under the talented and inspiring guidance of Dr. Anjana Felows, Reader and Major Advisor, Department of Home Science, Govt. Geetanjali Girls P.G. College, Bhopal. Her untiring supervision, resistant encouragement criticism has always been a constant source of my achievements. I am extremely indebted to her for being meticulous throughout investigation and preparation of this manuscript.

I also bestow my heartful thanks and gratitude to Mr. Arun Srivastava, Assistant Statistician, Department of Crop Physiology, Kanpur for not only helping me but also took keen interest throughout the course of investigation, had he not taken painstaking effort and inspiring attitude, the research work would have not been accomplished.

Words can never express the indebtedness but, I dare to take this opportunity to pay my sincere of gratitude and heartly thanks to Dr. Neelima Kunwar (D.Sc.) Associate Professor, Department of Extension Education and Communication Management, C.S. Azad University of Agriculture and Technology, Kanpur for stimulating my interest in carrying out this work.

From the inner core of my heart uncountable words of cordial veneration and gratitude are dedicated to the pious feet of my father Mr. Anjani Kumar Shukla and my mother Mrs. Rajani Shukla for their love, affection, good wishes, blessing and inspiration should by them for the achievements of my present educational assets.

From the very special corner of my heart I wish to record my indebtedness to my elder sister Mrs. Ruchi Mishra, my brother-in-law Mr. Arun Mishra, who have been always my strength.

I am deeply flooded with my emotions for my beloved younger sister Miss. Abhiruchi, for her constant love and support.

Suruchi Shukla

Contents

Introduction

"Violence against women is a manifestation of historically unequal power relations between men and women, which have led to domination over and discrimination against women by men and to the prevention of the full advancement of women"

(United Nations Declaration, 1993).

Violence affects the lives of millions of women, worldwide, in all socio-economic and educational classes. It cuts across cultural and religious barriers, impending the right of women to participate fully in society.

Domestic violence can be described as when one adult in a relationship misuses power to control another. It is the establishment of control and fear in a relationship through violence and other forms of abuse. The violence may involve physical abuse, sexual assault and threats. Sometimes its more subtle, like making someone feel worthless, not letting them have any money, or not allowing them to leave the home.

Domestic violence is not just hitting, or fighting, or an occasional argument. It's an abuse of power. The abuser tortures and controls the victim by calculated threats, intimidation and physical violence. Domestic violence occurs when a family member, partner or ex-partner attempts to physically or psychologically dominate another. Domestic violence often refers to violence between spouses, but can also include cohabitants and non-married intimate partner. Domestic violence occurs in all cultures; people of all races, ethnicities, religions and classes can be perpetrators of domestic violence. Domestic violence is perpetrated by and on, both men and women, and occurs in same sex and opposite sex relationship.

The U.S. office on violence against women defines domestic violence as a "Pattern of abusive behaviour in any relationship that is used by one partner to gain or maintain power and control over another intimate partner".

In children and family court advisory and support service in the *United Kingdom in its 'Domestic Violence Policy' uses domestic violence to refer to a range of violent behaviour defining it as : "Patterns of behaviour characterized by the misuse of power and control by one person over another who are or have been in an intimate relationship. It can occur in mixed gender relationships and same gender relationships and has profound consequences for the lives of children, individuals families and communities. It may be physical, sexual emotional or psychological. The latter may include intimidation, harassment, damage to property, threats and financial abuse.*

Forms of Domestic Violence

All forms of domestic abuse have one purpose to gain and maintain total control over the victim. Abusers use many tactics to exert power over their spouse or partner; dominance, humiliation, isolation, threats, intimidation, denial and blame. The form and characteristics of domestic violence and abuse may vary in other ways. Distinctions need to be made regarding types of violence, motives of perpetrators, and the social and cultural context. Violence by a person against their intimate partner is often done as a way for controlling 'their partner', even if this kind of violence is not the most frequent. Other types of intimate partner violence also occur, including violence between gay and lesbian couples, and by women against their male partners.

Physical Abuse

Physical abuse is abuse involving contact intended to cause feelings of intimidation, pain, injury, or other physical suffering or bodily harm.

Physical abuse includes hitting, slapping, punching, choking, pushing and other types of contact that result in physical injury to the victim. Physical abuse can also include behaviours such as denying the victim of medical care when needed, depriving the victim of sleep or other functions necessary to live, or forcing the victim to engage in drug/alcohol use against his/her will. It can also include inflicting physical injury onto other targets, such as children or pets, in order to cause psychological harm to the victim.

Sexual Abuse

Sexual abuse is common in abusive relationships. The National Coalition Against Domestic Violence reports that between one-third and one-half of all battered women are raped by their partners at least once during their relationship. Any situation in which force is used to obtain participation in unwanted, unsafe, or degrading sexual activity constitutes sexual abuse. Forced sex, even by a spouse or intimate partner with whom consensual sex has occurred is an act of aggression and violence. Furthermore, women whose partners abuse them physically and sexually are at a higher risk of being seriously injured or killed.

Categories of sexual abuse include :

1. Use of physical force to compel a person to engage in a sexual act against his or her will, whether or not the act is completed;

2. Attempted or completed sex act involving a person who is unable to understand the nature or condition of the act, unable to decline participation, or unable to communicate unwillingness to engage in the sexual act, e.g. because of underage immaturity, illness, disability, or the influence of alcohol or other drugs, or because of intimation or pressure; and
3. Abusive sexual contact.

Emotional Abuse

Emotional abuse (also called psychological abuse or mental abuse) can include humiliating the victim privately or publicly, controlling what the victim can and cannot do, withholding information from the victim, deliberately doing something to make the victim feel diminished or embarrassed, isolation the victim from friends and family, implicitly blackmailing the victim by harming others when the victim expresses independence or happiness, or denying the victim access to money or other basic resources and necessities.

Emotional/verbal abuse is defined as any behaviour that threatens, intimidates, undermines the victim's self-worth or self-esteem, or controls the victim's freedom. This can include threatening the victim with injury or harm, telling the victim that they will be killed if they ever leave the relationship, and public humiliation. Constant criticism, name-calling, and making statements that damage the victim's self-esteem are also common forms of emotional abuse. Often perpetrators will use children to engage in emotional abuse by teaching them to harshly criticize the victim as well. Emotional abuse includes conflicting actions or statements which are designed to confuse and create insecurity in the victim. These behaviours also lead the victim to question themselves, causing them to believe that they are making up the abuse or that the abuse is their fault.

Emotional abuse includes forceful efforts to isolate the victim, keeping them from contacting friends or family. This is intended to eliminate those who might try to help the victim leave the relationship and to create a lack of resources for them to rely on if they were to leave. Isolation results in damaging the victim's sense of internal strength, leaving them feeling helpless and unable to escape from the situation. Male privilege is often used to control victims and to maintain the perpetrator's power in the relationship (such as the concept of a man being 'head' of a household or defining a woman's role as submissive).

People who are being emotionally abused often feel as if they do not own themselves; rather, they may feel that their significant other has nearly total control over them. Women or men undergoing emotional abuse often suffer from depression, which puts them at increased risk for suicide, eating disorders, and drug and alcohol abuse.

Verbal Abuse

Verbal abuse is a form of abusive behaviour involving the use of language. It is a form of profanity that can occur with or without the use of expletives. Abusers may ignore, ridicule, disrespect, and criticize others consistently; manipulate words; purposefully humiliate; falsely accuse; manipulate people to submit to undesirable behaviour, make others feel unwanted and unloved; threaten economically; place the blame and cause of the abuse on others; isolate victims from support systems; harass demonstrate Jekyll and Hyde behaviours, either in terms of sudden rages or behavioural charges, or where there is a very different 'face' shown to the outside world *vs.* with victim. While oral communication is the most common form of verbal abuse, it includes abusive words in written form.

Financial Abuse

Financial abuse can take many forms, from denying you all access to funds, to making you solely responsible for all finances while handling money irresponsibly himself. Money becomes a tool by which the abuser can further control the victim, ensuring either her financial dependence on him, or shifting the responsibility of keeping a roof over the family's head on to the victim while simultaneously denying your ability to do so or obstructing you. Financial abuse can include the following like preventing you from getting or keeping a job, denying you sufficient housekeeping, having to account for every penny spent, denying access/to cheque book/ account, finances, putting all bills in your name, forcing you to beg or commit crimes for money, and spending child benefit on himself. The financial abuse includes :

(a) Deprivation of all or any economic or financial resources to which the aggrieved person is entitled under any law or custom whether payable under an order of a court or otherwise or which the aggrieved person requires out of necessity including, but not limited to, household necessities for the aggrieved person and her children, if any, stridhan, property, jointly or separately owned by the aggrieved person, payment of rental related to the shared household and maintenance;

(b) Disposal of household effects, any alienation of assets whether movable or immovable, valuables, shares, securities, bonds and the like or other property in which the aggrieved person has an interest or is entitled to use by virtue of the domestic relationship or which may be reasonably required by the aggrieved person or her children or her stridhan or any other property jointly or separately held by the aggrieved person; and

(c) Prohibition or restriction to continued access to resources or facilities which the aggrieved person is entitled to use or enjoy by virtue of the domestic relationship including access to the shared household.

CYCLE OF VIOLENCE

Stage One : Tension-Building

- Rather than using mutual communication, negotiation, or compromise to solve problems, violent individuals tend to rely on the use of force or coercion to get what they want.

- Typically, violence occurs after a build-up of tension in the relationship about issues which are not directly discussed or resolved.
- During this period, tension mounts, communication decreases, and both partners may feel tension, edgy, and jumpy.
- Arguments and criticism tend to increase during this period.

Stage Two : Violence

- After this build-up, physical violence may erupt over seemingly insignificant issues.
- Tension seems to be released, and often, the relationship seems to improve.

Stage Three : Seduction

- Perpetrators of violence often apologize, make promises to change, and pay special attention to their partners immediately following a violent incident.
- This period is sometimes referred to as the 'honeymoon period' because of the positive feelings resulting from the release of tension and the hope that things will change for the better.
- This kind of spontaneous change rarely occurs, however, because the underlying pattern of control and lack of communication and compromise has not changed.
- **Abuse** : The abuser lashes out with aggressive or violent behaviour. The abuse is a power play designed to show the victim 'who is boss'.
- **Guilt** : After the abusive episode, the abuser feels guilt, but not over what he's done to the victim. The guilt is

over the possibility of being caught and facing consequences.

- **Rationalization or excuses :** The abuser rationalizes what he's done. He may come up with a string of excuses or blame the victim for his own abusive behaviour—anything to shift responsibility from himself.
- **'Normal' behaviour :** The abuser does everything he can to regain control and keep the victim in the relationship. He may act as if nothing has happened, or he may turn on the charm. This peaceful honeymoon phase may give the victim hope that the abuser has really changed this time.
- **Fantasy and planning :** The abuser begins to fantasize about abusing his victim again, spending a lot of time thinking about what she's done wrong, and how he'll make her pay. Then he makes a plan for turning the fantasy of abuse into reality.
- **Set-up :** The abuser sets up the victim and puts his plan in motion, creating a situation where he can justify abusing her.

Cause of Domestic Violence

There are many different theories as to the causes of domestic violence. These include psychological theories that consider personality traits and mental characteristics of the perpetrator, as well as social theories which consider external factors in the perpetrator's environment, such as family structure, stress, social learning. As with many phenomena regarding human experience, no single approach appears to cover all cases.

(i) Psychological : In general, about 80 per cent of both court-referred and self-referred men in these domestic violence studies exhibited diagnosable psychopathology, typically personality disorders. Estimates of personality disorder in the general population would be more in the 15 –

20 per cent range. As violence becomes more severe and chronic, the likelihood of psychopathology in these men approaches 100 per cent. Psychological theories focus on personality traits and mental characteristics of the offender. Personality traits include sudden bursts of anger, poor impulse control, and poor self-esteem. Various theories suggest that psychopathology and other personality disorders are factors, and that abuse experienced as a child leads some people to be more violent as adults. Studies have found high incidence of psychopathy among abusers.

Dutton has suggested psychological profile of men who abuse their wives, arguing that they have borderline personalities that are developed early in life. Gelles suggests that psychological theories are limited, and points out that other researchers have found that only 10 per cent (or less) fit this psychological profile. He argues that social factors are important, while personality traits, mental illness, or psychopathy are lesser factors.

(ii) Behavioural : Behavioural theories draw on the work of behaviour analysis. Applied behaviour analysis uses the basic principles of learning theory to change behaviour. Behavioural theories of domestic violence focus on the use of functional assessment with the goal of reducing episodes of violence to zero rates. This programme leads to behaviour therapy. Often by identifying the antecedents and consequences of violent action, the abusers can be taught self control. Recently more focus has been placed on prevention and a behavioural prevention theory.

(iii) Social theories : Social theories contains the external factors of the offender's environment such as family structure which include resource theory, social stress, social learning and power and control theory.

(a) Resource theory : Resource theory was suggested by William Goode (1971). Women who are most dependent on the spouse for economic well-being. Having children to take

care or should they leave the marriage, increases the financial burden and makes it all the more difficult for them to leave. Dependency means that they have fewer options and few resources to help them cope with or change their spouse's behaviour.

Couples that share power equally experience lower incidence of conflict, and when conflict does arise, are less likely to resort to violence. If one spouse desires control and power in the relationship, the spouse may resort to abuse. This may include coercion and threats, intimidation, emotional abuse, economic abuse, isolation, making light of the situation and blaming the spouse, using children (threatening to take them away), and behaving as 'master of the castle'.

(b) Social stress : Stress may be increased when a person is living in a family situation, with increased pressures. Social stresses, due to inadequate finances or other such problems in a family may further increase tensions. Violence is not always caused by stress, but may be one way that some (but not all) people respond to stress. Families and couples in poverty may be more likely to experience domestic violence, due to increased stress and conflicts about finances and other aspects. Some speculate that poverty may hinder a man's ability to live up to his idea of 'successful manhood', thus he fears losing honour and respect. Theory suggests that when he is unable to economically support his wife, and maintain control, he may turn to misogyny, substance abuse, and crime as ways to express masculinity.

(c) Social learning theory : Social learning theory suggests that people learn from observing and modelling after other's behaviour. With positive reinforcement, the behaviour continues. If one observes violent behaviour, one is more likely to imitate it. If there are no negative consequences (e.g. victim accepts the violence, with submission), then the behaviour will likely continue. Often, violence is transmitted from generation to generation in a cyclical manner.

(d) Power and control : In some relationships, violence arises out of a perceived need for power and control, a form of bullying and social learning of abuse. Abusers' efforts to dominate their partners have been attributed to low self-esteem or feelings of inadequacy, unresolved childhood conflicts, the stress of poverty, hostility and resentment toward women (misogyny), hostility and resentment toward men (misandry), personality disorders, genetic tendencies and socio-cultural influences, among other possible causative factors. Most authorities seen to agree that abusive personalities result from a combination of several factors, to varying degrees.

An alternative view is that abuse arises from powerlessness and externalizing/projecting this and attempting to exercise control of the victim. It is an attempt to 'gain or maintain power and control over the victim' but even in achieving this it can't resolve the powerlessness driving it. Such behaviours have addictive aspects leading to a cycle of abuse or violence. Mutual cycles develop when each party attempts to resolve their own powerlessness in attempting to asserts control.

Duluth developed 'Power and Control Wheel' to illustrate this : it has power and control at the center, surrounded by the various techniques. The Wheel is a way of looking at the behaviours abuses use to get and keep control in their relationships. It is used to gain power and control over another person. Physical abuse is only one part of a system of abusive behaviours.

Abuse is Never a One Time Event

This chart uses the wheel to show the relationship of physical abuse to other forms of abuse. Each part shows a way to control or gain power :

- Coercion and threats
- Intimidation

- Emotional abuse
- Isolation
- Minimizing, denying and blaming
- Using children
- Economic abuse
- Male privilege

Dominance

Abusive individuals need to feel in charge of the relationship. They will make decisions for you and the family, tell you what to do, and expect you to obey without question. Your abuser may treat you like a servant, child, or even as his possession.

Humiliation

An abuser will do everything he can to make you feel bad about yourself, or defective in some way. After all, if you believe you're worthless and that no one else will want you, you're less likely to leave. Insults, name-calling, shaming, and public put-downs are all weapons of abuse designed to erode your self-esteem and make you feel powerless.

Isolation

In order to increase your dependence on him, an abusive partner will cut you off from the outside world. He may keep you from seeing family or friends, or even prevent you from going to work or school. You may have to ask permission to do anything, go anywhere, or see anyone.

Threats

Abusers commonly use threats to keep their victims from leaving or to scare them into dropping charges. Your abuser may threaten to hurt or kill you, your children, other family members, or even pets. He may also threaten to commit suicide, file false charges against you, or report you to child services.

Intimidation

Your abuser may use a variety of intimation tactics designed to scare you into submission. Such tactics include making threatening looks or gestures, smashing things in front of you, destroying property, hurting you pets, or putting weapons on display. The clear message is that if you don't obey, there will be violent consequences.

Denial and Blame

Abusers are very good at making excuses for the inexcusable. They will blame their abusive and violent behaviour on bad childhood, a bad day, and even on the victims of their abuse. Your abuser may minimize the abuse or deny that it occurred. He will commonly shift the responsibility onto you : Somehow, his violence and abuse is your fault.

Factors Responsible for Domestic Violence

There is no one single factor to account for violence perpetrated against women. Several complex and interconnected institutionalized social and cultural factors have kept women particularly vulnerable to the violence directed at them, all of them manifestations of historically unequal power relations between men and women.

Factors contributing to these unequal power relations include: socio-economic forces, the family institution where power relation are enforced, fear of and control over female sexuality, belief in the inherent superiority of males and legislation and cultural sanctions that have traditionally denied women and children on independent legal and social status.

Cultural ideologies—both in industrialized and developing countries—provide *'legitimacy'* for violence against women in certain circumstances. Religious and historical traditions in the past have sanctioned the chastising and beating of wives. The physical punishment of wives has been particularly sanctioned under the notion of entitlement and ownership of women. Male control of family wealth inevitably places decision making authority in male hands, leading to male dominance and proprietary rights over women and girls.

The concept of ownership in turn, legitimizes control over women's sexuality, which in many law codes has been deemed essential to ensure patrilineal inheritance. Women's sexuality is also tied to the concept of family honour in many societies. Traditional norms in these societies allow the killing of 'errant' daughters, sisters and wives suspected of defiling the honour of the family by indulging in forbidden sex, or marrying and divorcing without the consent of the family. By the same logic, the honour of a rival ethnic group or society can be defiled by acts of sexual violence against its women.

Excessive consumption of alcohol and other drugs has also been noted as a factor in provoking aggressive and violent male behaviour towards women and children. A survey of domestic violence in Moscow revealed that half the cases of physical abuse are associated with the husband's excessive alcohol consumption.

The isolation of women in their families and communities is known to contribute to increased violence, particularly if those women have little access to family or local organizations. On the other hand, women's participation in social networks has been noted as a critical factor in lessening their vulnerability to violence and in their ability to resolve domestic violence. These networks could be informal (family and neighbours) or formal (community organizations, women's self-help groups, or affiliated to political parties)."

Investigations by Human Rights Watch have found that in cases of domestic violence, law enforcement officials frequently reinforce the batterers' attempts to control and demean their victims. Even though several countries now have laws that condemn domestic violence when committed against a woman in an intimate relationship, these attacks are more often tolerated as the norm than prosecuted as laws... . In many places those who commit domestic violence are prosecuted less vigorously and punished more leniently than perpetrators of similarly violent crimes against strangers."

The factors are classified into four categories:

- Cultural
- Economic
- Legal
- Political

(i) Cultural

- Gender specific socialization
- Cultural definitions of appropriate sex roles
- Expectation of roles within relationship
- Belief in the inherent superiority of males
- Values that give men proprietary rights over women and girls
- Customs of marriage

(ii) Economic

- Women's economic dependence on men
- Limited access to cash and credit
- Discriminatory laws regarding inheritance, property rights, use of communal lands and maintenance after divorce of widowhood
- Limited access to employment in formal and informal sectors
- Limited access to education and training for women

(iii) Legal

- Lesser legal status of women either by written law/or by practice

- Laws regarding to divorce, child custody, maintenance and inheritance
- Legal definition of rape and domestic abuse
- Low levels of legal literacy among women
- Insensitive treatment of women of girls by police and judiciary

(iv) Political

- Under representation of women in power, politics, the media and in the legal and medical professions
- Domestic violence not taken seriously
- Notions of family being private and beyond control of the state
- Risk of challenge to status quo/religious laws
- Limited organization of women as a political force
- Limited participation of women in organized political system

Consequences of Violence

The consequences of violence are divide in four parts:

(i) ***Denial of fundamental rights :*** Perhaps the most crucial consequence of violence against women and girls is the denial of fundamental human rights to women and girls. International human rights instruments such as the Universal Declaration of Human Rights (UDHR), adopted in 1948, the Convention on the Elimination of All Forms of Discrimination Against Women (CEDAW), adopted in 1979, and the Convention on the Rights of the Child (CRC), adopted in 1989, affirm the principles of fundamental rights and freedoms of every human being. Both CEDAW and the CRC are guided by a broad concept of human rights that stretches beyond civil and political rights to the core

issues of economic survival, health, and education that affect the quality of daily life for most women and children. The two Conventions call for the right to protection from gender based abuse and neglect.

(ii) ***Human development goals undermined*** : There is a growing recognition that countries can't reach their full potential as long as women's potential to participate fully in their society is denied. Data on the social, economic and health costs of violence leave no doubt that violence against women undermines progress towards human and economic development.

(iii) ***Health consequences*** : Domestic violence against woman leads to far-reaching physical and psychological consequences, some with fatal outcomes. While physical injury represents only a part of the negative health impacts on women, it is among the more visible forms of violence.

Sexual assaults and rape can lead to unwanted pregnancies, and the dangerous complications that follow from resorting to illegal abortions. Girls who have been sexually abused in their childhood are more likely to engage in risky behaviour such as early sexual intercourse, and are at greater risk of unwanted and early pregnancies. Women in violent situations are less able to use contraception or negotiate safer sex, and therefore run a high risk of contacting sexually transmitted diseases and HIV/AIDS.

The impact of violence on women's mental health leads to severe and fatal consequences. Battered women have a high incidence of stress and stress-related illnesses such as post-traumatic stress syndrome, panic attacks, depression, sleeping and eating disturbances, elevated blood pressure, alcoholism, drug abuse, and low self-esteem. For some women, fatally depressed and demeaned by their abuser, there seems to be no escape from a violent relationship except suicide.

HEALTH CONSEQUENCES OF VIOLENCE AGAINST WOMEN

Non-fatal Outcomes

Physical Health Outcomes

- Injury (from lacerations to fractures and internal organs injury)
- Unwanted pregnancy
- Gynaecological problems
- STDs including HIV/AIDS
- Miscarriage
- Pelvic inflammatory disease
- Chronic pelvic pain
- Headaches
- Permanent disabilities
- Asthma
- Irritable bowel syndrome
- Self-injurious behaviours (smoking, unprotected sex)

Mental Health Outcomes

- Depression
- Fear
- Anxiety
- Low self-esteem
- Sexual dysfunction
- Eating problems
- Obsessive-compulsive disorder
- Post traumatic stress disorder

Fatal Outcomes

- Suicide
- Homicide

- Maternal mortality
- HIV/AIDS

(iv) ***Impact on children :*** Children who have witnessed domestic violence or have themselves been abused, exhibit health and behaviour problems, including problems with their weight, their eating and their sleep. They may have difficulty at school and find it hard to develop close and positive friendships. They may try to run away or even display suicidal tendencies.

Violence Against Women in Case Laws

- Section 304-B - dowry death
- Section 354 - Assault or criminal force to woman
- Section 366 - kidnapping abducting or inducing a woman
- Section 372 - selling minor for purposes of prostitution
- Section 376 - rape
- Section 376-A - intercourse by a man with his wife during separation
- Section 376-B - intercourse by public servant with woman in his custody
- Section 376-D - intercourse by any member of the hospital with any woman in that hospital
- Section 494 - remarriage
- Section 498 - enticing or taking away or detain a married woman
- Section 498-A - dowry cruelty.

Preventing Violence Against Women

Family violence prevention goes hand-in-hand with the recognition that family violence is a serious problem in our communities. Such recognition isn't easy. This is a problem that often goes unnoticed. Violence in families frequently remains invisible because family members are reluctant to report it. Professionals may not detect the presence of violence or they may fail to report it when they realize it has occurred. There are those who argue persuasively that is solutions to family violence are to be found among the various social ills that directly or indirectly influence its victims such as poverty, unemployment, and inadequate housing. However, societal-level solutions are often are difficult to describe and implement.

Most experts in the field emphasize the importance of preventing family violence rather than reacting to it after the fact. However, human service providers and community leaders have traditionally adopted a crisis management approach instead of developing needed preventive measures. As professionals we seem to be good at reporting and investigating, and not so good at treatment and prevention. Too many communities continue to direct the bulk of their resources towards responding to, rather than preventing, family violence.

Healthcare providers are receiving additional training that will help them respond more effectively to family violence. Also, training is taking place to promote interagency collaboration. When police, lawyers, and treatment providers work together, the improvement in outcomes is dramatic. Judges and district attorneys have a substantial role in the prevention of violence. It is important that the courts convey a clear message that family violence is unacceptable and that it will not be tolerated. A community that refuses to tolerate a behaviour is likely to produce fewer citizens who engage in that behaviour.

Preventing family violence begins with social awareness and the recognition that expertise, energy, and money will be needed to effectively address the conditions that produce family violence. With any problem, early detection and intervention are crucial to the prevention of more serious problems. The problem of family violence is no different. Recognizing that family violence is a serious problem in our communities, committing the necessary resources, identifying families at risk early on, and providing needed services are the heart of violence prevention.

Keeping in view the above facts, the present study has, therefore, been designed to investigate the effect of domestic violence on the life of farm women with the following specific objectives :

1. To study the socio-economic status of victim;
2. To ascertain the kinds of domestic violence in the study area;
3. To identify factors responsible for the domestic violence in the family;
4. To study the causes and consequences of violence on women; and
5. To evaluate the practicability of preventive measures.

JUSTIFICATION OF THE STUDY

The family is often equated with seek love, safety, security and shelter. But the evidence shows that it is also a place that imperils lives, and breeds some of the most drastic forms of violence perpetrated against women and girls.

Violence in the domestic sphere is usually perpetrated by males who are or who have been, in positions of trust and intimacy and power—husbands, boy friends, uncles, sons or other relative. Domestic violence is in most cases violence perpetuated by men against women. Women can also be violent, but their actions account for a small percentage of domestic violence.

Violence against women is often a cycle of abuse that manifests itself in many forms throughout their lives. Even at the very beginning of her life, a girl may be the target of sex selective abortion or female infanticide in cultures where son preference is prevalent. During childhood violence against girls may be include enforced malnutrition, lack of access to medical care and educational, incest, female genital malnutrition, early marriage and forced prostitution or bonded labour.

The present study was undertaken to examine the status, kinds and factors related to the domestic violence. This study will help to show the status of those women who are suffering from domestic violence in the society.

Review of Literature

The review of literature is the basis of most of the research. "The literature in any field forms the foundation upon which all future work is built". Review of related literature of the study has become an established practice of all research report but this should not be taken as mere practice or traditions in writing research process. Briefly it may be pointed out that review of related literature gives an insight into the problems. The important aspect of this tradition is that the researcher comes to know about the present position of the problem and also the explored and unexplored aspect of the problem. It was in view of these considerations that the investigator shifted the pages of journals, abstracts, so the different aspect of problem may be elaborated.

Liz Kelly (1998) has defined violence as "any physical, visual, verbal or sexual act that is experienced by the woman or girl at the time or later as a threat, invasion or assault, that has the effect of hurting her on degrading her and/or takes away her ability to contest an intimate contact".

United Nation Study (1998) according to this study, "the extent of violence against women in the home has been largely hidden and widely denied by communities that fear that an admission of its incidence will be an assault on the integrity of the family".

Ahuja (1998) defined the forms of violence were "slapping, kicking, tearing, hair pushing and pulling, hitting with an object, attempting to strangulate and threatening. Forms of psychological abuse were also found to exist for instance".

Stanko (1998) defined "domestic violence is a generic term, which refers to abusive and assaultive behaviour between intimates, among members of a household and or between former partners. Its most dominant form is man to woman within a partnership or former partnership".

Joanne Liddle (1998) said "any physical, visual, verbal or sexual act that is experienced by the person at the time or later as a threat, invasion or assault, that has the effect of hurting or disregarding or removing the ability to control one's own behaviour or an interaction, whether this be within the workplace, the home, on the streets or in any other area of the community".

Vernon J. Geberth (1998) defined "domestic violence defined as a pattern of behaviours involving physical, sexual, economic and emotional abuse, alone or in combination, by an intimate partner often for the purpose of establishing and maintaining power and control over the other partner. The origins of domestic violence are in social, legal and cultural norms, some historical and some current, including acceptance of violent behaviour by men as the heads of households. While domestic violence occurs in all types of intimate relationships, it is overwhelmingly a problem of violence perpetrated by men against women".

Memmot and Stacy (1999) said "domestic violence is a serious social issue which not only has profound effect on the individuals and families directly involved but also has a considerable social and economic impact on the community as a whole".

Tomita (1999) defined "economical abuse includes any behaviour that maintains power and control over finances, such as : preventing their partner from getting or keeping job".

Conference on Women (1999) has defined "violence against women as a physical act of aggression of one individual or group against another or others. Violence against women is any act of gender based violence which result in, physical, sexual or arbitrary deprivation of liberty in public or private life and violation of human rights of women in violation of human rights of women in situations of armed conflicts.

Sikri (1999) defined "sexual harassment of working women is primarily a problem faced by women, that men rarely face this problem and therefore it should be considered a form of sex discrimination".

Visaria (1999) defined "joint family tends to offer women some protection or act as a deterrent to husbands using physical force to subdue them".

Morrison and Orlando (1999) "moderate physical violence occurs when a women's partner slaps her, twist her arm, holds her against her will, or shoves her. These actions must have occurred fewer than times a year. If they occur more often, they fall into the next category. Severe physical violence occurs when a women suffers more than five acts of moderate physical violence in a year, or if her partner has kicked her, hit her with an object, burned her intentionally, cut her with a knife, or choked her; or if her partner's violent behaviour causes her injuries such as body aches, broken bones, loss of attention. Consciousness or any type of injury that requires medical attention. The two definitions are not mutually exclusive".

Ornaldo (1999) said that "domestic violence is an abuse of power perpetrated mainly (but not only) by men against women either in a relationship or after separation. Domestic violence takes a number of forms including physical and sexual violence, emotional and social abuse and financial deprivation. Many indigenous communities prefer the term family violence that includes all forms of violence within intimate and family relationship".

Sikri (1999) said that "unwanted sexual overtures, has the virtue of parsimony but necessarily concerns intentions and motivations, not just overt behaviour. Defining sexual harassment as unwanted sexual overtures has the same problem inherent in defining rape as unwanted sexual relations. In practice the woman has to prove that the sexual relations or the sexual overtures were unwanted".

Tjaden and Thoennes (2000) has been defined "domestic violence is a serious, preventable public health problem affecting more than 32 million Americans or more than 10 per cent of the U.S. population".

Roberts (2000) defined "domestic violence is an abuse of power perpetrated mainly by men against women both in a relationship or after separation. It occurs when one partner attempts physically or psychologically to dominate and control the other. Domestic violence takes a number of forms. The most commonly acknowledged forms are physical and sexual violence, threats and intimidation, emotional and social abuse and economic deprivation".

Williamson (2000) defined that "unwelcome sexual advances, requests for sexual favours and other verbal or physical conduct of a sexual nature constitute sexual harassment when this conduct explicitly or implicitly affects an individual's employment, unreasonably interferes with an individual's work performance, or creates an intimidating, hostile, or offensive work environment".

Women's Service Network (2000), "domestic violence is an abuse of power perpetrated mainly (but not only) by men against women in a relationship or after separation. Domestic violence takes a number of forms both physical and sexual violence; emotional and social abuse; and economic deprivation".

Quinn (2000) defined "psychological abuse is the willful infliction of mental or emotional anguish by threat, humiliation, or other verbal or non-verbal conduct. It is often associated with situations of power imbalance, such perhaps as the situations of abusive relationships and child abuse; however, it can also take place on larger scales, such as group psychological abuse, racial oppression and bigotry".

Newton (2001) defines that, "domestic violence can occur between adult family members who are not 'intimate' in the traditional sense, such as adult brothers and sisters, cousins, brothers-in-law, sisters-in-law, mothers and fathers-in-law for example consider elder abuse to be a form of domestic violence.

Snugg et al. (2001) defined domestic violence as "past or present physical and/or sexual violence between former or current intimate partners, adult household members, or adult children and a parent. Abused persons and perpetrators could be of either sex, and couples could be heterosexual or homosexual".

American Medical Association (2001) defines, intimate partner abuse as "the physical, sexual, and/or psychological abuse to an individual perpetrated by a current or former intimate partner, while this term is gender—neutral, women are more likely to experience physical injuries and incur psychological consequences of intimate partner abuse".

Lily Greenon (2002) "domestic violence has been recognized as a public issue. Domestic violence, also known as intimate partner violence is a concern because 1.5 million women are raped and/or physically assaulted by an intimate partner every year and domestic violence is the leading cause of injuries to women ages 15-44".

Jacket (2002) "among the many manifestations of the violations of the fundamental rights of women, domestic violence is one of the most vicious. It takes place behind closed doors, the very doors which are meant to protect women from the hazards of the outside world. It is nothing short of a form of a custodial violence and must be so recognized. Domestic violence must come out of the closet and be addressed".

Lynn Barkley Burnett (2002) said that "violence against women is a violation of human rights. It is one of the few phenomena which cuts across every imaginable cultural, political, socio-economic, ethnic, religious and educational boundary".

Beall (2002) defined, "physical attacks by the abuser is often accompanied by, or culminate in, sexual violence wherein the victim is forced to have sexual intercourse with the abuser or take part in unwanted sexual activity, including unprotected sex".

Fraser (2002) defines "financial abuse as a form of isolating the abused woman, financial abuse is also a control mechanism that limits the woman from becoming independent or looking for social supports. This type of abuse can manifest itself in behaviours.

Miller and Burstow (2002) defined "emotional abuse is one of the most prevalent forms of abuse of women by their intimate partners and its damage is unquestionably severe, undermining a woman's sense of worth, agency, and independence. Emotional abuse crosses all social classes, ethnic groups, sexual orientations and religious. The common dominators of abuser are personal, social and psychological not demographic".

Wechsler (2003), defined physical abuse, "the abuser's physical attacks or aggressive behaviour can range from bruising to murder. It often begins with what is excused as trivial contacts that escalate into more frequent and serious attacks. Physical abuse includes behaviours like : pushing, shoving, slapping, damaging property, or valued items, leaving partner in a dangerous place, refusing to provide assistance when their partner is sick or injured, attacking with weapons, etc.".

Lily Greenon (2003) defined "domestic violence has been recognized as a public issue. Domestic violence, also known as intimate partner violence, is a concern because 1.5 million women are raped and/or physically assaulted by an intimate partner every year and domestic violence is the leading cause of injuries to women ages 15-44".

Bedi (2003) said that domestic violence includes, harassment, maltreatment, brutality or cruelty and even the threat of assault-intimidation. It includes physical injury, as well as "willfully or knowingly placing or attempting to place a spouse in fear of injury and compelling the spouse by force or threat to engage in any conduct or act, sexual or otherwise, from which the spouse has a right to obtain". Confining or detaining the spouse against one's will or damaging property is also considered as acts of violence.

United Nation Declaration (2003) according to this "historically unequal power relations between men and women, which have led to domination over and discrimination against women by men and to the prevention of the full advancement of women, recognizing that violence against women is one of the crucial social mechanisms by which women are forced into a subordinate position compared with men".

Ramsey-Klawsnik, H. (2003) defined, "economical abuse that any behaviour that maintains power and control over finances, such as : preventing their partner from getting or keeping a job, making their partner ask for money for every expense, limiting partner's access to funds and knowledge of family finances, and controlling their funds.

Williamson (2004) said, "the spectrum of domestic violence (which, incidentally, has a high level of recidivism) may include psychological, physical, sexual, financial and emotional abuse which may manifest itself as physical injury, the deprivation of food, money or other resources, intimidation, humiliation and degradation, and may result in annedonia, pain, exhaustion, isolation, alienation, depression, fear and decreased levels of self-esteem, productivity and attentiveness. The law forbids any kind of violence".

Hoffman (2004) defined, "psychological or mental violence can include anything that impacts the mental health and well being of the partner, such as : name-calling, constant criticism, harassment, blaming the victim for everything, excessive possessiveness and jealousy, isolation from family and friends, intimidation and humiliation".

Gretchen E. Ely (2004) says that "domestic violence is a serious and neglected issue in immigrant communities, just as it is throughout the United States."

Lily Greenon (2004) "violence against women is widespread and may affect women of any age, class, race, religion, sexuality or ability. Factors which may increase women's vulnerability to some type of violence include age, disability and poverty. Across all forms of violence and abuse, women are most at risk from men they know".

Thomson Gale (2005) said, "domestic violence tends to be a pattern of behaviour used by one person in a relationship to control the other. The most frequently reported type of domestic violence is physical abuse such as hitting, punching, pushing, arm-twisting, biting, and use of a weapon. Other criminal forms include stalking; sexual abuse such as unwanted, forced sexual activity; emotional abuse which may include intimidation, mind games insults, torture, or threats of suicide; economic abuse such as withholding money or preventing the partner from obtaining or holding o job; and dating abuse which occurs even though the victim and abuser do not cohabitate. Domestic abuse may occur continuously or sporadically".

Nerenberg (2005) said that sexual assault is when an individual uses physical or psychological violence for sexual purposes. This type of assault may or may not be accompanied by physical injuries. There are different levels of sexual assault : sexual touching, sexual assault and aggravated sexual assault and sexual assault with weapon".

Desai (2006) said that "sexual harassment is nothing less than the showcasing of male dominance. Given an opportunity, such men (those committing sexual harassment) would try fulfilling their desire. However, it also not true that all cases of sexual harassment are such—where the accused is guilt of conceiving the intention of a sexual intercourse. But it also depends on each individual case and circumstances, because it may well be the case that the woman may also be at fault.

Soli Sorabjee (2006) defined sexual abuse "includes any conduct of sexual nature that abuses, humiliates, degrades or otherwise violates the dignity of woman".

Lockie (2007) refers "domestic violence as a pattern of behaviour that is used to gain or maintain power and control over an intimate partner".

Haytar (2007) defined "domestic violence—Impacts millions of people, children and adults alike, in the United States every year. Although domestic violence usually includes violent, physical attacks, it may include psychological, economic and sexual abuse, as well as attempts to isolate the partner.

Lee Williams (2007) defined "domestic violence occurs when a family member, partner or ex-partner attempts to physically or psychologically dominate another. Domestic violence often refers to violence between spouses, but can also include cohabitants and non-married intimate partners".

Fraser (2007) defined "domestic violence has been conceptualized as creating a pattern in which the central issue is control to create dependence, promote social isolation and inhibit a victim's reality testing".

Lily Greenon (2007) defined "violence is a learned behaviour that is usually passed on from one generation to next, unless efforts are made to interrupt the dysfunctional pattern. Intervention not only teached the partners more positive ways to resolve conflicts, but it teaches the more appropriate interaction patterns, thus the cycle of abuse can be stopped".

Kim Stuared (2007) said that "women abuse, is the physical, sexual, psychological and economical abuse of a person by her intimate partner whether they are married, common–law, or dating; current or former relationships; or same or opposite sex couples. Abuse of women is common society and can happen to people regardless of their culture, religion, age, sexual orientation, income, or education".

Desai (2007) defined sexual harassment and rape are two sides of the same coin. Both showcase the power of man to dominate that women. Both have one victim 'women'. Both are barbaric in nature; but many people extenuate sexual harassment to rape, just because the victims are not physically harmful, whereas in rape—the victim is ravished like an animal for the fulfillment of desire and lust of another man. Both have the same object to undermine the integrity of the victim, physically as well as mentally.

Lokie (2007) refers "domestic violence as a pattern of behaviour that is used to gain or maintain power and control over an intimate partner".

Haytar (2007) defined, "domestic violence impacts millions of people, children and adults alike, in the United States every year. Although domestic violence usually includes violent, physical attacks, it may include psychological, economic and sexual abuse, as well as attempts to isolate the partner.

Nandita Ṣaikia (2007) "rape is a crime involving forced sexual activity, usually including sexual penetration, against the will of the victim. Rape can occur in the context of ongoing domestic violence (where a partner sexually assaults another partner against that partner's will), but it may also be perpetrated by acquaintances (e.g., date rape) or by strangers".

U.S. Department of Justice (2007) reported that domestic violence divide into two types reciprocal violence, in which both partners are violent, and non-reciprocal violence in which one partner is violent. Physical abuse is abuse involving contact intended to cause feeling of intimidation, pair injury, or other physical suffering or bodily harm. Physical abuse including hitting, slapping, punching, chobing, pushing and other types of contact that result in physical injury to the victim. Physical abuse can also include behaviour such as denying the victim of medical care when needed, depending the victim of sleep or other function necessary to live or forcing the victim to engage in drug alcohol use against his/or will.

Carney et al. (2007) says that seek to describe violence in terms of gender is the amount of silence, fear and shame that results from abuse within families and relationship. Another is that abusive pattern can tend to seem normal to those who have lived in them for a length of time. Similarly, subtle forms abuse can be quite transparent even as they set the stage for further abuse seeming normal.

World Health Organization (2007) reported that domestic violence is a global issue reaching across national boundaries as well as socio-economic, cultural, racial and class distinctions. This problem is not only widely dispersed geographically but its incidence is also extensive, making it a typical and accepted behaviour. Domestic violence is wide-spread, deeply ingrained and has serious impacts on women's health and well being. Its continued existence is morally indefensible. Its cost to individuals, to health system and to society is enormous. Yet no other major problem of public health has been so widely ignored and so little understood.

Kannabiran and Menon (2007) say that violence against women in India is of potential interest to anyone who is engaged in the area of women's issues and especially to those who are interested in women's issues in India. It discusses a spectrum of issue related to violence against women belonging to different castes, classes, religions, and sexual orientations in India although parallels could possibly be drawn to similar population groups in the rest of South Asia as well.

Jena (2007) says that if any society is seen within its right perspective, it is only a women who is matrix of its social fabric. Women constitute half the population of world. In India they are referred as better half, still women had worst deal at the ends of the society and are exploited in all possible manner.

Amnestry International (2007) reported that violence against women is a violation of human rights that cannot be justified by any political, religious or cultural claim. A global culture of discrimination against women allows violence to occur daily and with impunity.

American Academy of Family Physicians (2008) defines, "violence against a partner is a crime in all states. Each year, at least 4 million women are abused in this country. Abuse happens to people of all races, ages, incomes and religions. People who are hurt by their partners, parents or guardians do not cause the abuse. Alcohol and drugs do not cause abuse, although they can make the violence worse. Abuse can begin, continue and even increase during pregnancy".

Shorey et al. (2008) says that behavioural theories draw on the work of behaviour analysts. Applied behaviour analysis uses the basic principles of learning theory to change behaviour. Behavioural theories of domestic violence focus on the use of functional assessment with the goal of reducing episodes of violence to zero rates. The programme leads to behaviour therapy. Recently more focus has been placed on prevention and a behavioural prevention theory.

Moore et al. (2008) says that violence against women, especially by intimate partner, is a serious public health problem that is associated with physical, reproductive and mental health can sequences. Even though most societies prescribe violence against women. The reality is that violations against women rights are often sanctioned under the garb of cultural practices and norms, or through misinterpretation of religious tends.

Walby and Myhill (2008) says that violence against women includes, but should not be limited to physical, sexual and psychological domestic violence (battering, sexual violence in the family, marital rape female genital mutilation and other traditional practices harmful to women, non spousal violence). Violence in the community (rape, sexual, abuse and/or harassment at the work place, educational institutions or elsewhere, traffing in women and forced prostitution) and violence perpetrated or condoned by the state.

Sreenivasulu (2008) say that one of the major factors which block the universal realization of human right goal is violence. Particularly, women by reasons of violence against them are denied of full enjoyment of their human rights. In fact, international standard recognize violence against women and other forms of gender based prosecution as violations of fundamental and universal human rights. Women are exposed to acts of violence in the community (e.g. rape, sexual harassment).

Misra (2008) says that violence against women in any form is a violation of the right of equality. Among the many manifestation of the violations of the violations of the fundamental right of a women, domestic violence is one of the most vicious. Domestic violence is undoubtedly a human right issue and serious deterrent to development.

Times of India (2008) reported that even the ancient epics the Ramayana and Mahabharata depicts that during those days family conflicts and violence were prevalent. In puranic verses one finds the mention of violence against the women. So the different literatures available reveal that women were subjected to all kinds of humiliation and indignities. Not much have changed even today women are not feeling safe and secured in their homes and in the family. The homes where women are living are the dens of terror and horror.

Dissiz and Sahin (2008) says that violence against women and domestic violence is perceived and private and remains mostly hidden. Especially, due to the belief that what happen at home, stay at home is prevalent among women being subjected to domestic violence, it has taken a long time for it to emerge as a social issue.

Gelles (2008) says that violence is not a new thing for centuries human being have been violent one towards another. We as humans have to deal with different types of violence in every day life and some types of violence that we many experience are child abuse, spousal abuse or domestic violence stalking in some way may be classified as type of violence. It is in human nature to do violence one or another way domestic violence happens between individual who are dating, couples that are married separated or divorced, also domestic violence occur in heterosexual as well gay and lesbian relationship. All social, religious, ethic groups experienced domestic violence in one or another way.

Thompson et al. (2009) says that violence against women by male partners and ex-partners is a major public health problem, resulting in injuries and other short term and long term consequences, including mental illness and complications of pregnancy. Exposure of children to domestic violence results in emotional, behavioural and health problem.

UNIFEMS (2009) say violence against women and girls is one of the most widespread violations of human rights. It can include physical, sexual, psychological and economic abuse, and it cuts across boundaries of age, race, culture, wealth and geography. It takes place in the home, on the streets, in schools, the workplace in farm fields, refugee camps, during conflicts and crises. It has many manifestations—from the most universally prevalent forms of domestic and sexual violence, to harmful practices, abuse during pregnancy, so called honour billings and other types of femicide.

Sharma (2009) reported that is hardly anything to celebrate for women in India on International Women's Day, where instances of gender discrimination and violence are only increasing by the day. Experts say things cannot improve much unless there is substantial progress on socio-economic empowerment of women.

Singh et al. (2009) say that domestic violence against women is a widespread problem. However, its actual extent is difficult to measure. It may be very much higher than that the reports indicate because many instances of domestic violence against women are not reported. The research studies and surveys conducted by individual generally produce a higher estimates of violence than officials records. However, they are also assumed to under-estimate the actual extent of domestic violence against women. For a variety of reasons, women may fail to report violence that takes place in the family.

Womenhealth.gov (2009) reported that violence and abuse affect all kinds of people everyday. It doesn't matter what race or culture you come from. How much money you have, how old you are, of if you have a disability. Violence against does not discriminate. Above can be physical, mental or emotional. Violence against women in any form is a crime, whether the abuser is a family member someone you date : a current or post spouse, boy friend, or girl friend, can acquaintance or a stranger.

Gattordo (2009) say that women are half of the world's population and seventy experience some sort of violence by men in their lifetime. Violence against women is not an isolated incident. It occurs every day across every continent and knows no boundaries. The global conviction rate for rape is only five per cent of alleged attacks. In reality, women are still stigmatized and stereotyped and in many cases, unable to gain access justice.

Barua (2009) says that violence against women is common in most of the societies across the world. Though this is a frequent occurrence, but it is often regarded as mundane in our daily life and set aside as obscured and neglected phenomenon. Many women are subjected to physical or mental violence at different part of their lives and they often suffer in isolation and in silence in their domestic or occupational environment. Only a few episodes of severe and unusual violence are brought before public attention.

Smith and Segal (2010) say that domestic violence and abuse can happen to anyone, yet the problem is often overlooked, excused, or denied. This is especially true when the abuse is psychological, rather than physical. Emotional abuse is often minimized yet it can leave deep and lasting scars.

The Organisation for Economic Co-operation and Development (2010) reported that physical, sexual and psychological violence strikes women in epidemic proportions worldwide. It crosses every social and economic classes, every religion, race and ethnicity. From domestic abuse to rape as a weapon of war, violence against women is a gross violation of their human rights. Not only does it threaten women's health and their social and economic well-being, violence also towards global efforts to reduce poverty.

Oshodi (2010) says that domestic violence should not happen to anyone, in any place or at any time but it does. It is a relational vice that is endemic across all societies within and outside countries of Africa. It is generally a form of maltreatment that threatens the safety and health of the abused.

Issac (2010) say that violence against women is not only happening day-to-day life but also becoming a universal phenomenon. And it's always unfortunable to learn that every morning many women are in a long queue. Even within the third world countries, it's more common in the rural and backward areas and hence women are more prone to violence and vulnerable than those who are in the urbanized and developed regions.

3

Profile of the Study Area

Prior to discuss the findings of the study on "Causes and consequences of violence on women and the practicability of preventive measures", it is essential to sketch briefly the salient features.

Origin of the Name of the District

The district of Lucknow is named after the city of Lucknow, which is situated almost in the centre of the district. The origin of the name 'Lucknow' is not definitely traceable, and whatever traditions are available, are of extremely doubtful historical authenticity. Lucknow formed a part of the ancient kingdom of Kosal, and there is a tradition that the town was named in honour of Rama's brother, Lakshmana as Lakhanpuri which was corrupted into Lukhnau and later to its present designation of Lucknow. To the north-west of the town there is a mound, which is still called the Lakshmana Tila and lends support to this tradition. The story that the town is named after an ahir or milk-seller named Lakhna, who as a result of the spiritual blessings of a Muslim saint, had become rich and founded the town, is apocryphal and is hardly worthy of any credit. Even the *Ain-i-Akbari,* while dealing with the *Sarkar* of Lucknow as a part of the *Suba* of Avadh, does not throw any light on the origin of the name of Lucknow.

Location, General Boundaries, Total Area and Population of the District

The district of Lucknow formed the central part of the province of Avadh and was the headquarters of the *Sarkar* of Lucknow in the *Suba* of Avadh, in the time of Akbar. The district lies between the parallels 26°30′ and 27°10′ north latitude and 80°30′ and 81°13′ east longitude. The district is an irregular quadrilateral with the city and cantonment of Lucknow forming nearly the centre. It is bounded in the north by the district of Sitapur, on the east by that of Bara Banki, on the south by that of Raebareli and on the north-west and the south-west by the districts of Hardoi and Unnao, respectively. Except in a part in the south and south-west, the boundaries of the district can hardly be called natural, and appear to have been fixed arbitrarily for administrative convenience; the river Sai on the south and south-west forming the natural boundary for a short distance only. Some villages belonging to the Lucknow district still lie across the river. Sai to the north of the Lucknow-Kanpur Road, while some villages of district Unnao lies on the Lucknow side of the river Sai. It is understood that there is a proposal under consideration to rectify this anomaly and to transfer to the district of Unnao those villages in pargana Bijnor, which lie south of the river Sai, and to assign to Lucknow those villages of district Unnao, which lies between the river Sai and the present boundary of the district.

Area

With the exception of the district of Rampur, Lucknow is the smallest district in point of area in Uttar Pradesh. The area of the district on the basis of the professional survey by the survey of India, works out to 6,24,896 acres which is equivalent to 976.4 square miles. This is the area mentioned in the latest Census Report of 2001. The area mentioned in the various records of the Land Revenue Department cannot be relied upon, as it appears that they did not take into consideration the area occupied by the city and cantonment of Lucknow, which were not surveyed during the settlement and record operations. The results of the only reliable guide in this matter.

Population

The total population of the district according to the 2001 census was 59,68,795 of which the urban population accountable for 23,20,961 and the female population was 10,91,688 and the male was 12,29,273.

CLIMATE

Observatories

There are two observatories in the district, one at Amausi aerodrome, under the charge of a Meteorological Officer and the other at the Central Drug Research Institute, Chhatar Manzil, under the charge of its Director. In addition to these there are rain-gauge stations in all tahsil headquarters under the charge of the Tahsildar.

Seasons

The district is situated in the sub-tropical region and its climate can be said to be of sub-tropical monsoon type. It avoids the parching drought and the opposite extremes of heat and cold which are experienced in the Punjab. It is said that seasonality is the keynote of Indian climate and the three seasons—the rainy, the cold and the hot—are well marked off. The first commences with fair regularity in the middle of June and continues till the end of September, but as the monsoon from the Bay of Bengal sweeps over the Uttar Pradesh, the commencement of the rainy season may be early as the beginning of June or as late as the first or second week of July. The cold weather extends from early October to the end of February. March is a transitional month. The third season extends over the remaining months of the year. In this season the sun gradually moves towards the north and consequently the temperature begins to rise, and so it gradually merges into the hot weather with high temperature and dry westerly winds.

Temperature and Humidity

In winter the temperature is controlled by two factors :

(*i*) the slanting rays of the sun during winter; and

(*ii*) the development of anti-cyclone conditions in northern India.

The following table *(See on next page)* shows the mean maximum and mean minimum monthly temperatures with the highest and the lowest temperatures ever recorded in the district.

Communication Facilities

Of the early history of the district of Lucknow not much is known with a degree of authenticity. It was only during the mediaeval period that Lucknow acquired an importance, being the capital of the Lucknow *Sarkar* in the time of Akbar, and later, as the capital of the *Suba* of Avadh. The city of Lucknow is situated on the banks of the Gomati, on the direct trade routes across the Ganga and from the western part of Avadh to districts across the Gomati and the Ghagra, right up to the foothills of the Nepal tarai. It was on the direct route form the eastern districts of U.P. from Jaunpur to Delhi. It must, however, be stressed that the conception of roads then was not the same as now. The roads were well marked but hardly made *pakka* to say nothing of the modern developments. They could, therefore, be considered to be fair-weather roads, suitable for wheeled traffic, horses and men. There was no fast traffic in those days, and journeys were performed usually by short stages. The records of the administration of Avadh under the Nawabs were destroyed during the struggle of

Month	Mean daily max. temperature in		Mean daily min. temperature in		Highest max. temp. recorded		Lower min. temp. recorded in	
	°F	°C	°F	°C	°F	°C	°F	°C
January	73.9	23.4	47.1	8.4	86.0	30.2	35.0	1.67
February	78.6	25.9	51.4	10.8	95.0	35.0	35.0	1.67
March	90.8	32.7	60.6	15.9	106.0	41.2	45.0	7.22
April	101.4	38.8	70.8	21.6	114.0	45.6	55.0	12.75
May	105.4	40.8	78.3	25.8	117.0	47.2	64.0	17.8
June	100.2	39.0	81.7	27.7	119.0	48.9	67.0	13.9
July	92.4	33.5	79.5	26.4	114.0	45.6	72.0	22.2
August	90.5	32.6	78.6	25.9	102.0	39.0	72.0	22.2
September	91.9	33.4	76.5	24.8	103.0	39.2	64.0	17.8
October	91.4	33.1	65.5	19.2	104.0	40.0	52.0	11.1
November	83.9	28.9	54.1	12.3	94.0	34.5	42.0	5.55
December	75.9	24.4	47.3	8.5	92.0	33.2	35.0	1.57
Annual Average	**89.7**	**32.2**	**66.0**	**19.2**	**119.0**	**48.5**	**35.0**	**1.67**

1857, and the reports of the British authorities after 1857 are the only available records.

Road Transport

The usual conveyance used appears to have been the palanquins, carried on the shoulders of the men, and carriages drawn either by horses or by bullocks, horses and elephants were the favourite modes of transport for men, but with the improvement in the roads the conveyances also changed. The one-horse ekkas and tangas were the usual means of transport for the middle class and the cultivators both for passenger traffic as well as for carriage of goods from and to the bazaars. The bullock carts still continue to bring the cultivators' produce to the market, but for purposes of trade, the railway and the motor-trucks have supplanted all slow-moving traffic. They are both fast and cheap. The rich men of the city used to keep horse carriages, or open landaus and the sprightly little gigs for going about in the city. For the middle class and the poor, the horse-tongas and the ekkas had a suffice. The stately landaus have more or less vanished and few people keep horses or can afford to do so. The rich merchants, big zamindars, high officials and successful professional men all use motor-cars. The middle class persons, employees of Government and other offices and the tradesmen use bicycles. The motor scooter has also made its appearance on the roads of Lucknow city but they are still very few. Persons, who do not own any transport of their own, depend on the Government city bus service or the cycle rickshaw of which there seem to be very many. Small tradesmen, barbers, washermen, milkmen and others depend entirely on the bicycle for completing their daily round.

National and State Highways

The total mileage of national and provincial highways passing through the district is 125 miles 2 furlongs and 509 feet. This also includes those portions of national highways which pass through the Municipal area and are maintained by the P.W.D. The expenses for the maintenance of the national highways are made from the grants of the Central Government whereas the State Government provides funds for the provincial roads. A part of the national highways is constructed of cement concrete while the rest is made of tar macadam. The average width of the provincial highways is 12′ and that of national highways is 22′. On all these roads, roadside avenues provide shade for travellers, and are now being looked after by the Forest Department.

National Highways

1. Lucknow–Jhansi Road
2. Lucknow–Goarkhpur Road
3. Lucknow–Bareilly road

Provincial Highways

1. Lucknow–Varanasi Road
2. Lucknow–Sultanpur Road
3. Lucknow–Hardoi Road
4. Beni–Harauni–Tirwa Road
5. Machchhi Bhavan Bye–pass Road
6. Sitapur City Branch Road
7. Kaiser Bagh Road
8. University Road
9. River Bank Road
10. Husainabad Trust Road
11. K.K. College Road
12. Bakshi-ka-Talab-Asthi Border Road
13. Lady Milles Road (Road at the back of Ministers' Residence Nos. 1–5 on Cassels Road)
14. Cantonment Branch Road

Industries

Lucknow has long been famous for its industries, especially the cottage industries. As early as the first half of the 17th century Avadh's Calico commanded a ready market in London and in 1640 the English East India Company had established a factory at Lucknow for the supply of Calico pieces woven at Daryabad Khairabad and other places. Later on the munificent and benevolent patronage was afforded to these industries by the Nawabs of Avadh. It was the centre to which flocked all the tradesmen once the imperial majesties at Delhi had fallen on evil days. Poets and priests, artists and craftsmen all came to reside in the city of Lucknow. The influx of these people produced changes in the pattern of living and led to the establishment of certain peculiar characteristics of the Lucknow school of arts. Lucknow was well known for its splendours and all the travellers coming to this city have mentioned this fact in their memories. Those who were dazzles by the splendours of Lucknow were Hodge, Archer and Mundy. All of them were unanimous as regards the pomp and pageantry that they had witnessed at the time of their visits to this city.

Selected Sample of Lucknow District

Lucknow is well developed district. Lucknow is divided in different zones. out of this four zones selected in this study. 60 respondents were selected from each zone. Thus, 240 respondents were selected in the study area.

Research Methodology

This chapter deals with the research procedures applied in conducting the present study. For convenience, the research methodology has been discussed under the following three sub-heads:

1. Research design
2. Variables and their Operationalization
3. Data gathering procedure and statistical techniques used

1. Research Design

It comprises of the following sub-parts:

(*i*) Locale of the study

(*ii*) District under study

(*iii*) Selection of the area

(*iv*) Selection of respondents

(*v*) Pilot study

(*vi*) Pre-testing of instruments

(i) Locale of the study : Uttar Pradesh was chosen as locale of the study. This was done with the intension that U.P. is a major state of the country.

(ii) District under study : Lucknow district was purposively selected for this study as the researcher hailed from this place. This helped the investigator to collect the necessary information accurately and timely. The researcher, being from the same place could easily have dialogues and discussions with respondents during pilot study and final data collection.

(iii) Selection of the Area : Lucknow district comprises of different zones. Out of which four zones were randomly selected.

(iv) Selection of Respondents : A list of females was prepared separately for each zone. The respondents were selected randomly from each. Thus, in all 240 respondents were selected for study purpose in age groups (21–45 years).

(v) Pilot study : Prior to finally deciding the title of the project a pilot survey of the area was conducted. This gave an idea about the place of the study and nature of the samples that could be drawn and type of aspects and problems, which could be explored out.

(vi) Pre-testing of instruments : Before collecting the necessary data from the finally selected sample of 240 elderly 60 females was identified other than those included in the final sample of respondents. These 60 women were interviewed with the help of schedules and questionnaires developed for collecting the data. This helped the investigator in making necessary changes in the instruments to be finally used their wording and composition.

2. Variables and their measurements

(i) Independent variables

(a) Age : The chronological age of respondents at the time of investigation was taken. All respondents were listed

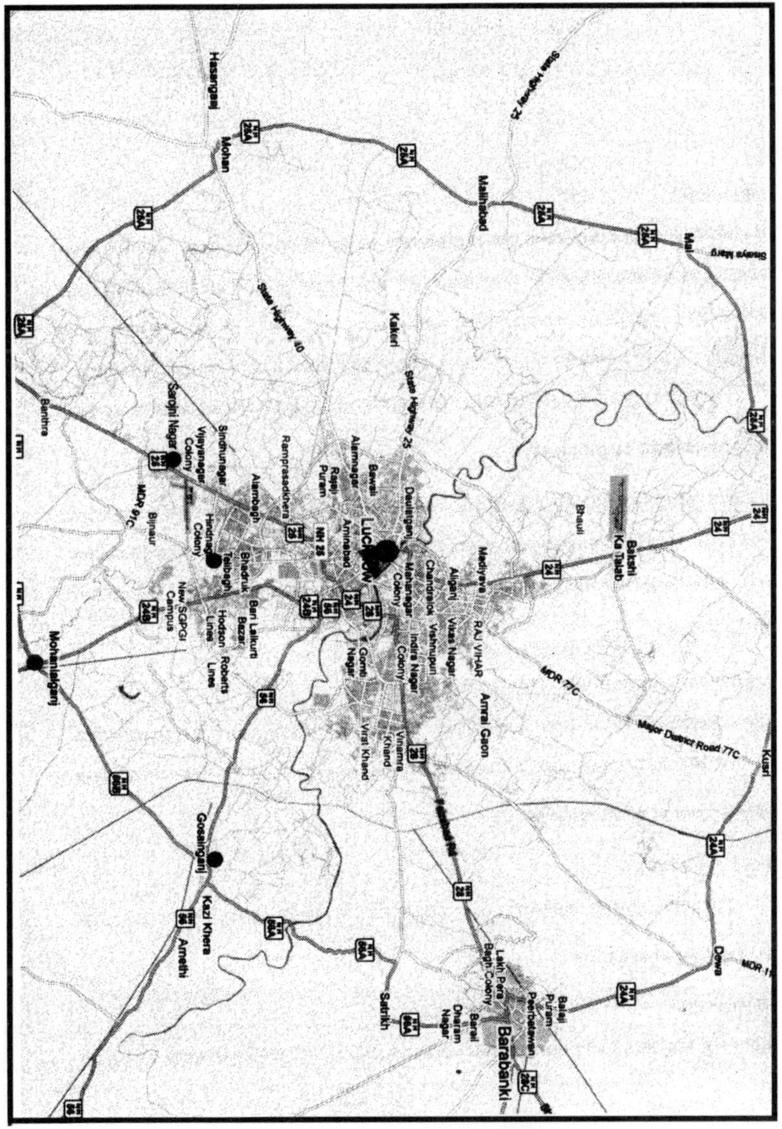

Map 4.1 : Map of Lucknow

according to following age groups and given the scores as follows:

Age-group (years)	Score assigned
(*a*) 21 – 29	1
(*b*) 29 – 37	2
(*c*) 37 – 45	3

(b) Educational qualification : Education was operationalized as the number of years of formal education obtained by the respondents. Scores assigned to different categories.

Educational qualification	Score assigned
Upto Intermediate	1
Graduate	2
Post Graduate & above	3

(c) Caste : Caste of the respondents in the study was measured on the basis of response of women to which they belong, i.e. in terms of upper caste, middle caste and lower caste. The scores were assigned as:

Caste	Score assigned
Upper	1
Middle	2
Lower	3

(d) Religion : The selected area was having mostly Hindu religion and some are Muslim. The following scoring pattern was adopted

Category	Score assigned
Hindu	1
Muslim	2
Sikh	3
Christian	4

*(e) **Female occupation** :* This was measured on the basis of the scores allotted to different family occupation in the socio-economic status scale.

Female Occupation	Score assigned
Service	1
Business	2
Housewife	3

***(f) Monthly income of the respondent* :** Income was referred to as the monthly income received by the respondent. It is measured in term of rupees. The score were assigned as:

Monthly income (Rs.)	Score assigned
upto 5,000	1
5,000 – 10,000	2
10,000 – 15,000	3
15,000 and above	4

(g) Family structure

Type of Family	Score assigned
Nuclear	1
Joint	2

(h) Social participation

Social participation	Score assigned
Social worker	1
Club member	2
Organisation member	3
No participation	0

(ii) Dependent variables

(a) Violence : Violence is physical force exerted for the purpose of violation, damaging or abusing and that is what

society at large recognizes violence. The word violence also includes the concept of discrimination exploitation, upholding of unequal economic and social structure and creation of an atmosphere of terror, violence is produced.

(b) Domestic violence : Domestic violence is an abuse of power perpetrated mainly by men against women in a relationship or after separation. Domestic violence takes a number of forms both physical and sexual violence; emotional and social abuse and economic deprivation. Domestic violence occurs in all cultures; people of all races, religions and classes.

(c) Cause : A cause is an agent or condition that permits the occurrence of an effect or leads to a result.

(d) Consequences : Consequences are outcomes negative or positive of a person's action. By their nature, they gauge our behaviour because we as humans strive for positive outcomes or consequences. There are two types of consequences : natural and logical. Both of these types can be positive or negative.

(e) Practicability : That may be practiced or performed; capable of being done or accomplished with available means or resources; feasible, as, practicable method; a practicable aim; a practicable good.

(f) Preventive measures : Measures carried out prior to the execution of the project which prevent previously identified environmental impacts specific practices for the prevention of disease or mental disorders in susceptible individuals or populations. Primary prevention is to be distinguished from secondary prevention, which is the prevention of complications or after effects of a drug or amelioration of the after effects of disease.

(g) Addiction : Addiction has been defined with regard solely to psychoactive substances (for example alcohol, tobacco and other drugs) which cross the blood-brain barrier once ingested, temporary altering the chemical milieu of the brain. A chronic relapsing condition characterized by compulsive

drug-seeking and abuse and by long-lasting chemical changes in the brain. Addiction is the same irrespective of whether the drug is alcohol, amphetamines, cocaine, heroin, marijuana, or nicotine. Every addictive substance induces pleasant states or relieves distress.

(h) Reaction : The force which a body subjected to the action of a force from another body exerts upon the latter body in the opposite direction.

(i) First aid : First aid is like being the first responder. First aid is the initial care that's given to the victim before medically trained personnel arrive, or before the victim arrives at a health care center.

(j) Power and control : Power is the rate of doing work or energy transmitted, or amount of energy required or extended for a given unit of time. Power or authority to check or restrain; restraining or regulating influence; superintendence; government; as, children should be under parental control.

3. Data Gathering Procedure and Statistical Techniques Used

(i) Preparation of Interview schedule : The methodology used to collect the information for the present study consist of interview based on with the help of interview schedule. This schedule was based on available authentic literature and was further verified by subject experts. Schedule consisted four parts namely A, B, C and D.

Part A consisted of socio-economic background of selected respondents. Information regarding kinds of domestic violence was collected in the part B of the schedule. Factor responsible for the domestic violence were collected in the part C in the schedule. Information regarding causes and consequences of violence were recorded in part D.

(ii) Data collection : The necessary evidences were collected in line with the objectives of the study. All the 240 respondents

were inclusively approaches by the researcher. By personal contact, all the respondents were interviewed with the help of the structured schedule developed for the study.

Hypotheses

Ho : There is no relationship between factors for the domestic violence and independent variables.

Ho : There is no relationship between causes and consequences of violence and independent variables.

(iii) Period of Data collection : The data collection was initiated from August 2009 to March 2010.

(iv) Statistical analysis : The following statistical techniques have been applied in the analysis of data.

1. Percentage : Single comparisons were made on the basis of the percentage, for drawing percentages, the frequency of a particular cell was multiplied by 100 and divided by total number of respondents in that particular category to which they belonged.

$$\text{Percentage} = \frac{\text{The sum of all the responses}}{\text{Total number of all the responses}} \times 100$$

2. Weighted mean : All the items are not of equal importance. At the time they are given proper weights according to their relative importance, and then the average which is calculated on the basis of these weight is called weighed average of the weighted mean.

$$\text{Weighted mean} = \frac{W_1X_1 + W_2X_2 + W_3X_3 + ...W_nX_n}{W_1 + W_2 + W_3 ....W_n}$$

$$= \sum_{i=1}^{n} \frac{W_iX_i}{W_i}$$

3. Correlation coefficient : Karl Pearson has given a coefficient of correlation for the measurement of linear relationship, which exists between two variables. If X and Y are two variables and if $E(X, Y) \neq 0$ then correlation coefficient (r) is

$$r = \frac{\text{Cov. (X, Y)}}{\sqrt{\text{Var. (X). Var. (Y)}}}$$

or

$$= \frac{\Sigma xy}{\Sigma x^2 \cdot \Sigma y^2}$$

where,

$$\Sigma \text{xy} = \left[\Sigma XY - \frac{\Sigma X \Sigma Y}{n}\right]$$

$$\Sigma x^2 = \left[\Sigma X^2 - \frac{(\Sigma X)^2}{n}\right]$$

$$\Sigma y^2 = \left[\Sigma Y^2 - \frac{(\Sigma Y)^2}{n}\right]$$

and n = Sample size

Here, one variable is dependent on other. For testing the significance of correlation coefficient (r), t test is applied. Degree of lack of relationship or coefficient of alienation is measured as :

$$K = \sqrt{1 - r^2}$$

5

Findings, Result and Discussion

The empirical results and its discussion have been presented in this chapter. For the purpose of convenience, the findings of the study have been sub-divided under the following heads :

1. Socio-economic status of victim;
2. Kinds of domestic violence in the study area;
3. Factors responsible for the domestic violence in the family;
4. Causes and consequences of violence on women;
5. Practicability of preventive measures.

I. SOCIO-ECONOMIC STATUS OF VICTIM

Age

Table 5.1*(See on page 58)* shows that distribution of women respondents according to age group, maximum 49.2 per cent women belonged to 29 to 37 years age group whereas, 28.3 per cent women respondents belonged to 37 to 45 years age-group. Minimum 22.5 per cent women were belonged to 21 to 29 years age group. Violence were slapping, kicking, tearing, hair pushing and pulling, hitting with an object, attempting to strangulate and threatening in 21 to 45 years age-group.

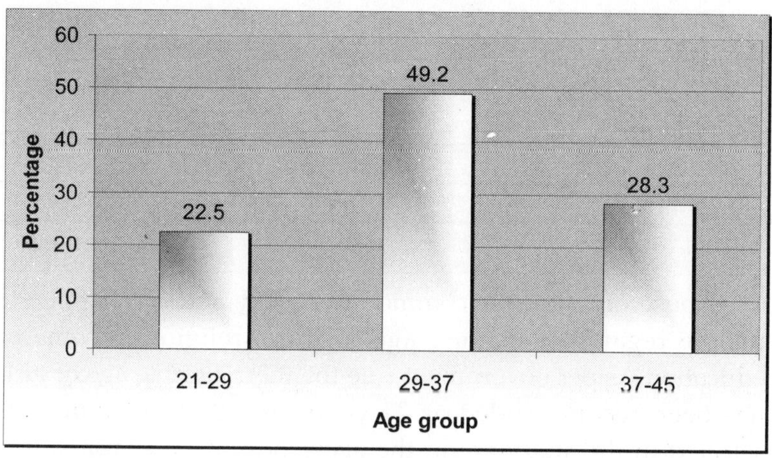

Fig. 5.1 : Distribution of women according to age group

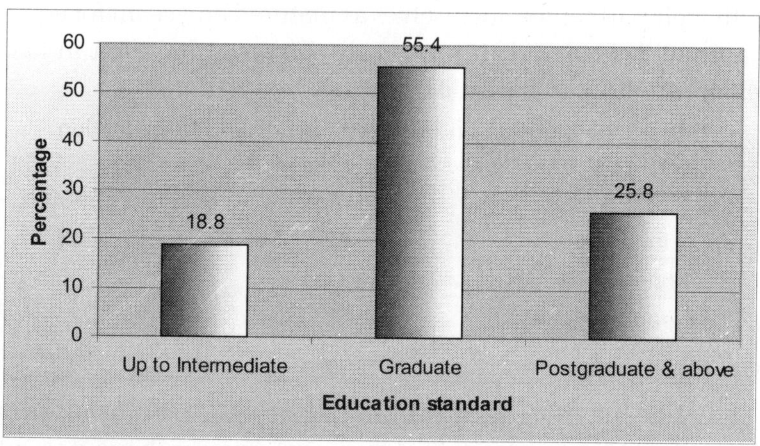

Fig. 5.2 : Distribution of women according to education

Table 5.1 : Distribution of women according to age group

Age group (years)	Frequency	Per cent
21 – 29	54	22.5
29 – 37	118	49.2
37 – 45	68	28.3
Total	**240**	**100.0**

Abuse of women is common in society and can happen to people regardless of their age, culture, religion, income or education.As per government rule the merriageable age of girls has been recommended as 21 years. So all the respondents selected in the study are in the age-group of 21-45 years. It is obvious that domestic violence is also found in this age group. However, in the present study, the highest 49.2 per cent cases of domestic violence have been found in the age group of 29-37 years. In this age group females after spending 5 to 10 years with their partner feel themselves as matured and claim for equal status with husband in the family. This results often in bad relations with partner in life.

Table 5.2 : Distribution of women according to education

Education	Frequency	Per cent
Up to Intermediate	45	18.8
Graduate	133	55.4
Post graduate & above	62	25.8
Total	**240**	**100.0**

Table 5.2 reveals that distribution of respondents according to education, 55.4 per cent women have passed graduate whereas, 25.8 per cent women respondents have passed postgraduate and above. Minimum 18.8 per cent women respondents have passed only Intermediate poor and or illiterate. These women have managed to mobilize hundreds of other women, raised resources, designed

strategies and forced policy makes to revise laws and policies. Women need to be empowered through education.

There seems to be no effect of education on domestic violence, because in the modern scenario, even after being empowered and educated, girls to tolerage the husband's cruelties like beating, addition with alcohol, having extra-marital relations and fighting on even small issues due to the fear from the society that the domestic issues may become public. They do tolerate all these up to a limit. However, illiterate women behave just reverse. They do not have fear of society and never felt sorry in putting their problem of violence in front of others. Number of examples can be cited like the fearless exposing character of playback singer Udit Narain by first wife and cases of wives of many politicians etc.

Table 5.3 : Distribution of women according to caste

Case	Frequency	Per Cent
Upper	142	59.2
Middle	67	27.9
Lower	31	12.9
Total	**240**	**100.0**

Table 5.3 indicates that distribution of women as per caste, 59.2 per cent women respondents have upper caste whereas 27.9 per cent women belonged to middle caste. 12.9 per cent women respondents belonged to lower caste. Violence is a learned behaviour that is usually passed on from one generation to next, unless efforts are made to interrupt the dysfunctional pattern.

Poverty alcoholism and mental illness all are further risk factors, and violence against women also is shaped by class, sexuality and other social divisions. It has been seen in the study that most of the domestic violence has been found among lower caste families because both the partners are mostly illiterate and they do not have the fear of society. However, now-a-days domestic violence is increasing among

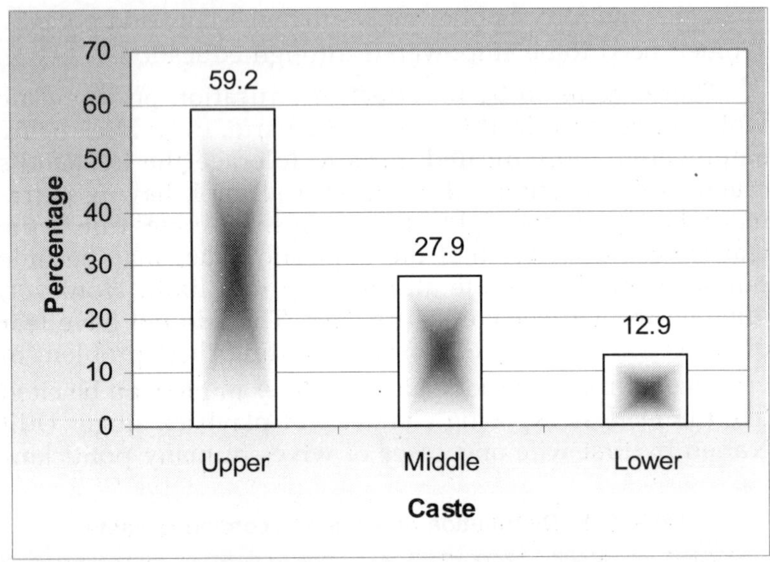

Fig. 5.3 : Distribution of women according to caste

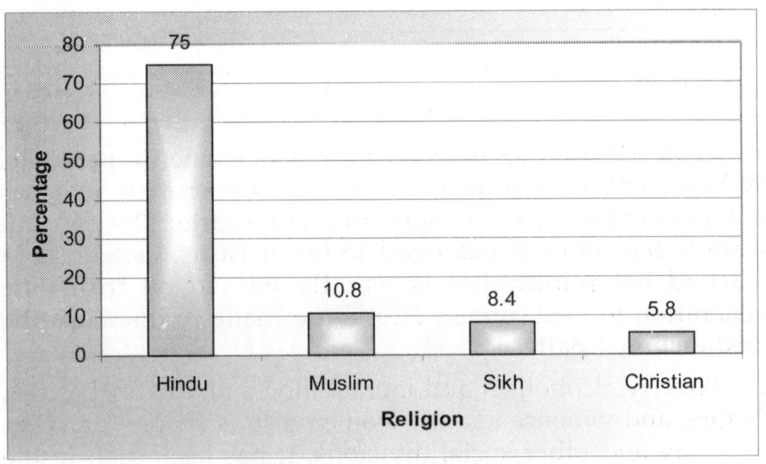

Fig. 5.4 : Distribution of women according to religion

middle class families too, due to professional tension, poor economic condition, high ambitiousness, lack of patience and extra marital relations.

Table 5.4 : Distribution of women according to religion

Religion	Frequency	Per Cent
Hindu	180	75.0
Muslim	26	10.8
Sikh	20	8.4
Christian	14	5.8
Total	**240**	**100.0**

Table 5.4 shows that distribution of women according to religion, 75.0 per cent women belonged to Hindu religion whereas 10.8 per cent women belonged to Muslim category. 8.4 per cent women respondents belonged to Sikh religion whereas 5.8 per cent Christian. Religion plays an important role in emotional or psychological abuse to chip away at feelings of self-worth and independence.

Traditions respondents the beliefs, values and way of thinking of a social group. Tradition as a social custom passed down from one generation to another through the process of socialization. Every religion have thin own tradition and beliefs. Most of the domestic violence has been found in Hindu families due to religious and social restrictions. As per Islamic rules, 4 marriages are legal in Muslim families and business group dominates in Muslim community. They do not posses qualities of high ambition, illiteracy rate is also very high.

Table 5.5 : Distribution of women according to family

Family	Frequency	Per cent
Nuclear	142	59.2
Joint	98	40.8
Total	**240**	**100.0**

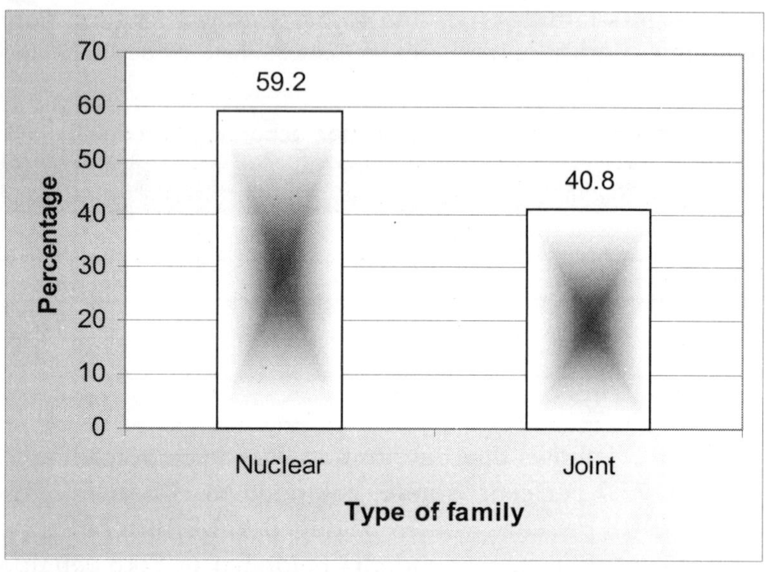

Fig. 5.5 : Distribution of women according to type of family

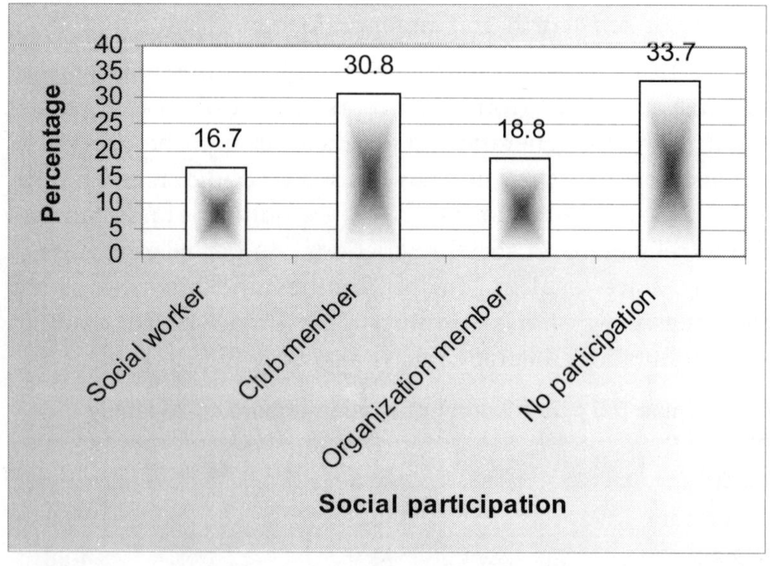

Fig. 5.6 : Distribution of women according to social participation

Table 5.5 shows that distribution of women respondents according to type of family, 59.2 per cent women respondents from nuclear family whereas 40.8 per cent women from joint family system. Now-a-days joint family system disintegrate into nuclear family system. In urban areas joint family system convert into nuclear family system while in rural areas it become slow. Domestic violence are less in joint family system due to the fear of older persons are shyness. However, 10 per cent cases have been reported in such families where older ones are conservative, greedy and aggressive.

Table 5.6 : Distribution of women according to social participation

Social participation	Frequency	Per Cent
Social worker	40	16.7
Club member	74	30.8
Organization member	45	18.8
No participation	81	33.7
Total	**240**	**100.0**

Table 5.6 shows that distribution of women according to social participation, 30.8 per cent women respondents were club member in various clubs whereas 18.8 per cent women have joined organization membership. 16.7 per cent women have social worker but she faced abuses and violence with their partner. 33.7 per cent women have no participation and not a member of any organization.

Table 5.7 : Distribution of women according to occupation

Occupation	Frequency	Per Cent
Service	136	56.7
Business	42	17.5
Housewife	62	25.8
Total	**240**	**100.0**

Cycle of Violence

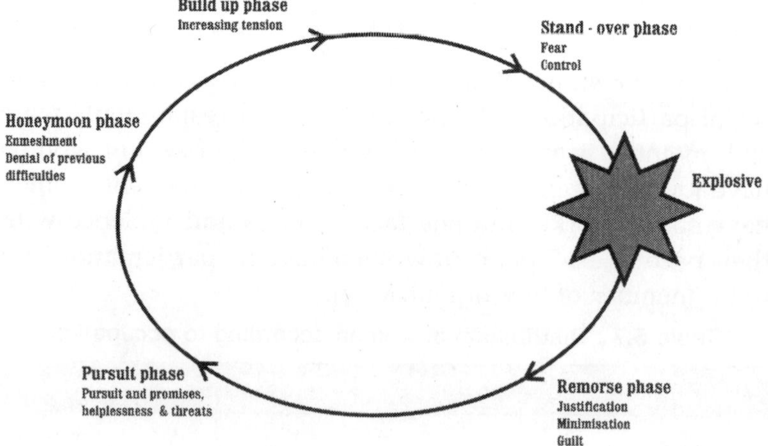

Cycle of Violence

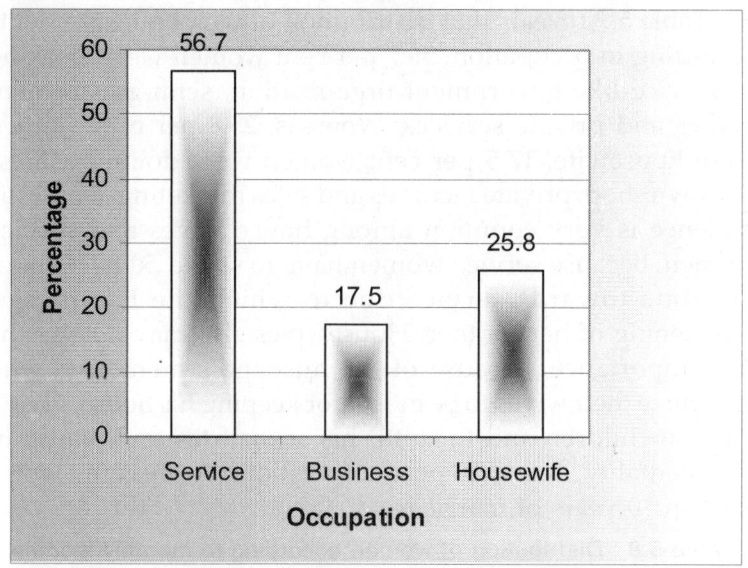

Fig. 5.7 : Distribution of women according to occupation

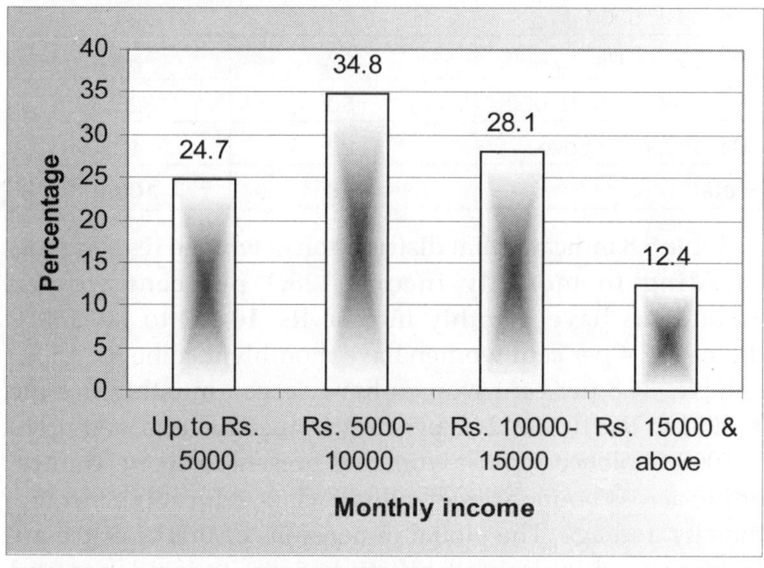

Fig. 5.8 : Distribution of women according to monthly income

Table 5.7 reveals that distribution of women respondents according to occupation, 56.7 per cent women were working in service like government organization, semi-government bodies and private services. Whereas, 25.8 per cent women were housewife. 17.5 per cent women were doing business like own shop, private factories and sales marketing. Domestic violence is very common among house wives and service women, because service women have to spend 50 per cent of her time towards service due to which she has to face threatening of her partner. Housewives also may not get the due importance, because of the husband's mentality, who recognize their wives to be meant for keeping his house, giving birth to children and to fulfill his sexual desire. Because of this mentality, nearly 50 per cent relationships become worse even in 10 years of marriage.

Table 5.8 : Distribution of women according to monthly income

Monthly income	Frequency	Per Cent
Up to Rs. 5000	44	24.7
Rs. 5000 – Rs. 10,000	62	34.8
Rs. 1000 – Rs. 15,000	50	28.1
Rs. 15000 & above	22	12.4
Total	**178**	**100.0**

Table 5.8 indicates that distribution of women respondents according to monthly income, 28.1 per cent women respondents have monthly income Rs. 10,000 to Rs. 15000 whereas 12.4 per cent women have monthly income Rs. 15000 & above. 34.8 per cent women have earned monthly income Rs. 5001 to Rs. 10,000. 24.7 per cent women have earned up to Rs. 5000. Violence against women is present in every country, cutting across boundaries of culture, class, education, income, ethnicity and age. The global dimensions of this violence are alarming, as highlighted by studies on its incidence and prevalence.

The social and economic costs of violence against women are enormous and have ripple effects throughout society. Women may suffer isolation, inability to work, loss of wages, lack of participation in regular activities, and limited ability to care for themselves and their children. If cases where women earn more, her husband fails to do much violence because, he consider her as a earning resource, which fulfills his family economic desires.

Table 5.9 : Awareness of type of domestic violence by respondents

Type of violence	Yes	No	Scores	Rank
Physical abuse	55 (22.9)	185 (77.1)	1.23	V
Sexual abuse	43 (17.9)	197 (82.1)	1.18	VI
Emotional abuse	105 (43.7)	135 (56.3)	1.44	II
Economic abuse	56 (23.3)	184 (76.7)	1.23	V
Verbal abuse	111 (46.3)	129 (53.7)	1.46	I
Psychological abuse	68 (28.3)	172 (71.7)	1.28	IV
Spousal abuse	79 (32.9)	161 (67.1)	1.33	III

Table 5.9 reveals that distribution of women respondents according to domestic violence, 43.7 per cent women have faced emotional abuse, both verbal or non-verbal. Emotional or psychological abuse such as name calling, blaming and shaming, isolation and controlling behaviour also fall under emotional abuse. 23.3 per cent women respondents faced economic abuse like denying all access of funds, money becomes a tool by which the abuser can further control the victim, ensuring either her financial dependence on him. Household necessities for the aggrieved person and her children, property, jointly or separately owned by the aggrieved person, payment of rental related to the shared household and maintenance. 22.9 per cent women have faced physical abuse in any act of violence on the victim and can include slapping, kicking, shoving, choking, pinching, pulling

hair, burning and beating etc. Physical abuse is the use of physical force against someone in a way that injures or endangers that person.

17.9 per cent women have faced sexual abuse can involve excessive jealousy, calling sexually derogatory names, criticizing and forcing unwanted sexual act, sadistic sexual acts, forcing sex after physical assault, taking unwanted sexual photos and forcing sex when ill or tired.

Physical abuse is far worse than emotional abuse, since physical violence can send you to the hospital and leave you with scars. But, the scars of emotional abuse are very real, and they run deep. In fact, emotional abuse can be just as damaging as physical abuse—sometimes even more so. Furthermore, emotional abuse usually worsens overtime, often escalating to physical battery. 46.3 per cent respondents have aware about verbal abuse whereas 32.9 per cent respondents faced spousal abuse.

Domestic violence and abuse can happen to anyone, yet the problem is often overlooked, excused, or denied. This is especially true when the abuse is psychological, rather than physical. Emotional abuse is often minimized, yet it can leave deep and lasting scars.

Domestic abuse, also known as spousal abuse, occurs when one person in an intimate relationship or marriage tries to dominate and control the other person. Domestic abuse that includes physical violence is called domestic violence.

Domestic violence and abuse does not discriminate. It happens among heterosexual couples and in same-sex partnerships. It occurs within all age ranges, ethnic backgrounds, and economic levels. And while women are more commonly victimized, men are also abused—especially verbally and emotionally. The bottom line is that abusive behaviour is never acceptable, whether it's coming from a man, a woman, a teenager, or an older adult. You deserve to feel valued, respected, and safe.

Physical abuse is abuse involving contact intended to cause feelings of intimidation, pain, injury, or other physical suffering or bodily harm.

Physical abuse includes hitting, slapping, .punching, choking, pushing, and other types of contact that result in physical injury to the victim. Physical abuse can also include behaviours such as denying the victim of medical care when needed, depriving the victim of sleep or other functions necessary to live or forcing the victim to engage in drug/ alcohol use against his/her will. It can also include inflicting physical injury onto other targets, such as children or pets, in order to cause psychological harm to the victim.

Sexual abuse is common in abusive relationships. The National Coalition Against Domestic Violence reports that between one-third and one-half of all battered women are raped by their partners at least once during their relationship. Any situation in which force is used to obtain participation in unwanted, unsafe, or degrading sexual activity constitutes sexual abuse. Forced sex, even by a spouse or intimate partner with whom consensual sex has occurred, is an act of aggression and violence. Furthermore, women whose partners abuse them physically and sexually are at a higher risk of being.

In many countries sexual assault by a husband on his wife is not considered to be a crime; a wife is expected to submit. It is thus very difficult in practice for a woman to prove that sexual assault has occurred unless she can demonstrate serious injury.

The report of the Special Rapporteur noted that light sentences in sexual assault cases send the wrong message to perpetrators and to the public at large; that female sexual victimization is unimportant.

Sexual harassment in the workplace is a growing concern for women. Employers abuse their authority to seek sexual favours from their female co-workers or subordinates, sometimes promising promotions or other forms of career advancement or simply creating an untenable and hostile work environment. Women who refuse to give into such unwanted sexual advances often run the risk of anything from demotion to dismissal.

Emotional abuse (also called psychological abuse or mental abuse) can include humiliating the victim privately or publicly, controlling what the victim can and cannot do, withholding information from the victim, deliberately doing something to make the victim feel diminished or embarrassed,, isolating the victim from friends and family, implicitly blackmailing the victim by harming others when the victim expresses independence or happiness, or denying the victim access to money or other basic resources and necessities.

Emotional/verbal abuse is defined as any behaviour that threatens, intimidates, undermines the victim's self-worth or self-esteem, or controls the victim's freedom. This can include threatening the victim with injury or harm, telling the victim that they will be killed if they ever leave the relationship, and public humiliation. Constant criticism, name-calling, and making statements that damage the victim's self-esteem are also common forms of emotional abuse. Often perpetrators will use children to engage in emotional abuse by teaching them to harshly criticize the victim as well. Emotional abuse includes conflicting actions or statements which are designed to confuse and create insecurity in the victim. These behaviours also lead the victim to question themselves, causing them to believe that they are making up the abuse or that the abuse is their fault.

Verbal abuse is a form of abusive behaviour involving the use of language. It is a form of profanity that can occur with or without the use of expletives.

Abusers may ignore, ridicule, disrespect, and criticize others consistently; manipulate words; purposefully humiliate; falsely accuse; manipulate people to submit to undesirable behaviour, make others feel unwanted and unloved; threaten economically; place the blame and cause of the abuse on others; isolate victims from support systems; harass; demonstrate Jekyll and Hyde behaviours, either in terms of sudden rages or behavioural changes, or where there is a very different 'face' shown to the outside world *vs.* with victim.

While oral communication is the most common form of verbal abuse, it includes abusive words in written form.

Economic abuse is when the abuser has control over the victim's money and other economic resources. In its extreme (and usual) form, this involves putting the victim on a strict 'allowance', withholding money at will and forcing the victim to bet for the money until the abuser gives them some money. It is common for the victim to receive less money as the abuse continues. This also includes (but is not limited to) preventing the victim from finishing education or obtaining employment, or intentionally squandering or misusing communal resources.

Many women are forced into prostitution either by their parents, husbands or boy friends—or as a result of the difficult economic and social conditions in which they find themselves. They are also lured into prostitution, sometimes by 'mail-order bride' agencies that promise to find them a husband or a job in a foreign country. As a result, they very often find themselves illegally confined in brothels in slavery-like conditions where they are physically abused and their passports withheld.

Most women initially victimized by sexual traffickers have little inkling of what awaits them. They generally get a very small percentage of what the customer pays to the pimp or the brothel owner. Once they are caught up in the system there is practically no way out, and they find themselves in a very vulnerable situation.

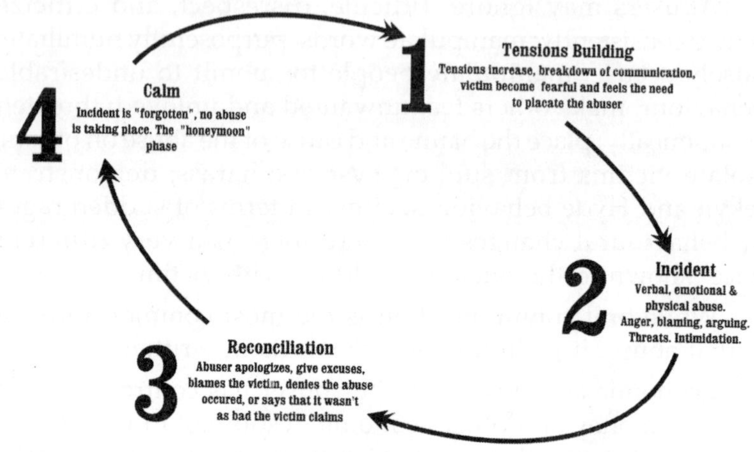

Cycle of Abuse

Many women and girl children are trafficked across borders, often with the complicity of border guards. In one incident, five young prostitutes burned to death in a brothel fire because they had been chained to their beds. At the same time, sex tours of developing countries are a well-organized industry in several European and other industrialized countries.

Table 5.10 : Type of abuse faced by Respondents

Type of abuse	Frequency	Per Cent
Verbal abuse	136	56.7
Emotional abuse	69	28.7
Sexual abuse	68	28.3
Spousal abuse	59	24.6
Physical abuse	38	15.8
Psychological abuse	47	19.6

The perusal of Table 5.10 reveals that respondents were faced types of abuse, 56.7 per cent respondents were faced verbal abuse whereas 28.7 per cent respondents have facing emotional abuse in daily life. 24.6 per cent respondents have faced spousal abuse whereas 28.3 per cent respondents were suffering from sexual abuse. 19.6 per cent respondents were suffering from psychological abuse whereas 15.8 per cent women faced physical abuse.

There are many signs of an abusive relationship. The most telling sign is fear of your partner. If you feel like you have to walk on eggshells around your partner—constantly watching what you say and do in order to avoid a blow-up-chances are your relationship is unhealthy and abusive. Other signs that you may be in an abusive relationship include a partner who belittles you or tries to control you, and feelings of self-loathing, helplessness, and desperation.

The perusal of Table 5.11 *(See on page 73)* reveals that distribution of partner according to addiction, 50.0 per cent male have taking Gutkha whereas 34.2 per cent respondents partners were taking alcohol. 5.8 per cent males were found to be addicted with Bhang, whereas 16.7 per cent male have addicted to smoking like cigarette/bidi and 7.9 per cent male have taking drugs. 26.2 per cent male partner have always suspicious about female sex and 17.1 per cent male partner have suffering form psyche.

Table 5.11 : Distribution of male partner according to addiction

Addiction	Frequency	Per Cent
Wine	82	34.2
Drug	19	7.9
Gutkha	120	50.0
Cigarette/Bidi	40	16.7
Bhang	14	5.8
Suspicious person	63	26.2
Psychic person	41	17.1

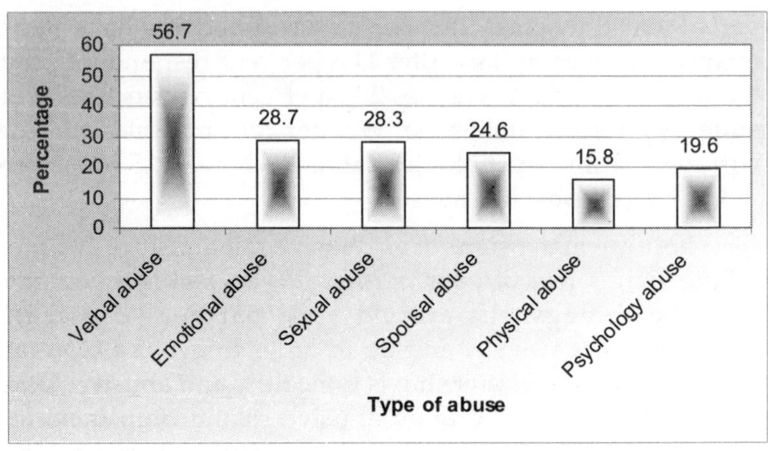

Fig. 5.9 : Respondents faced by type of abuse

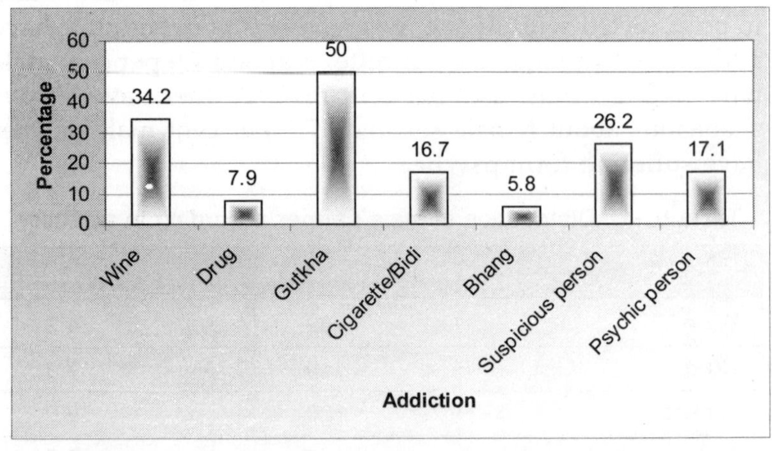

Fig. 5.10 : Distribution of male partner according to addiction

Domestically violent men have a number of alcohol related problems. However, alcohol and drug can't be seen as casual factors for family violence, but more or precipitating ones. Although alcohol and drug may not cause violence, they definitely contribute to its lethality.

There is general correlation between alcohol consumption and violence toward a spouse or partner. They sometimes occur together. But does drinking actually cause abuse in a relationship? Researchers and other experts warn against jumping to the conclusion that it does.

Alcohol does not and cannot make one person abuse another. Many authorities explain that "men who batter frequently use alcohol abuse as an excuse for their violence. They attempt to rid themselves of responsibility for the problem by blaming it on the effects of alcohol.

Table 5.12 : Effect of reaction on women

Reaction	Adoption	Percentage
Silent	100	41.7
Argue	36	15.0
Protect her	40	16.7
React same	10	4.2
Leave home	39	16.2
Beauty	8	3.3
Others	7	2.9
Total	**240**	**100.0**

Although most writers focus on men as abusers of women, research also indicates that women abuse men about as often. And there's no reason to believe that alcohol causes women to abuse men. Husbands who are addicted with wine, drugs, cocaine or using cigarette or bidi, they get irritated early, become aggressive and loose patience easily. These acts hurts their wives. In the study, 26.2 per cent husbands are found to be mysterious, whose wives do not expect the kind of behaviour from their counterparts, 17.7 per cent husband were found psychic, who kept doubt and threat their wives. These actions put their wives always in a fearful environment.

The perusal of Table 5.12 shows that reaction of women respondents during violence, 41.7 per cent women have reacted silent during violence, they were taking all types of abuse and violence silently not given any objection and argue whereas 16.7 per cent women have protect herself during violence and various abuse. They were defended herself with their partner. 16.2 per cent women respondents leave home after violence and abuses, they were choosing safe side but it is not a solution to stop the violence while 15.0 per cent women have taking defend side by argue to protect himself, some educated women were taking this type of reaction. 4.2 per cent reacted same during violence.

Women can experience a wide range of reactions after being sexually assaulted and there is no one pattern of responsc. Some women respond immediately, others may have delayed reactions. Some women are affected by the assault for a long time whereas others appear to recover rather quickly.

In the early stages, many women report feeling shock, confusion, anxiety, and/or numbness. Sometimes women will experience feelings of denial. In other words, they may not fully acknowledge what has happened to them or they may downplay the intensity of the experience. This reaction may be more common among women are assaulted by someone they know.

In the first few days and weeks following the assault, it is very normal for a woman to experience intense and sometimes unpredictable emotions. She may have repeated strong memories of the event that are difficult to ignore, and nightmares are not uncommon. Women also report having

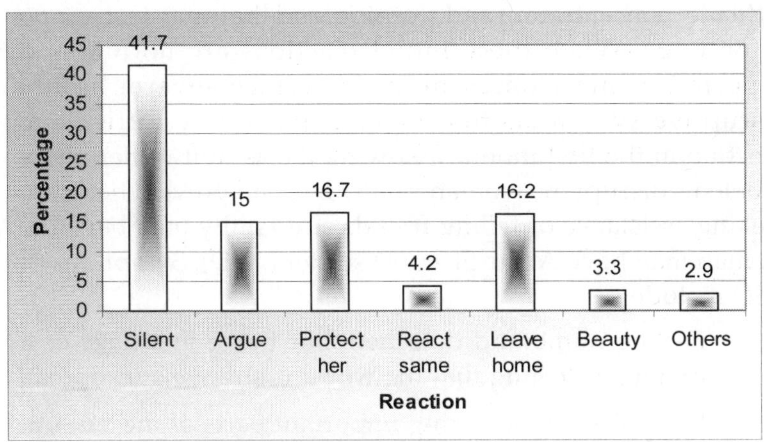

Fig. 5.11 : Effect of reaction on women

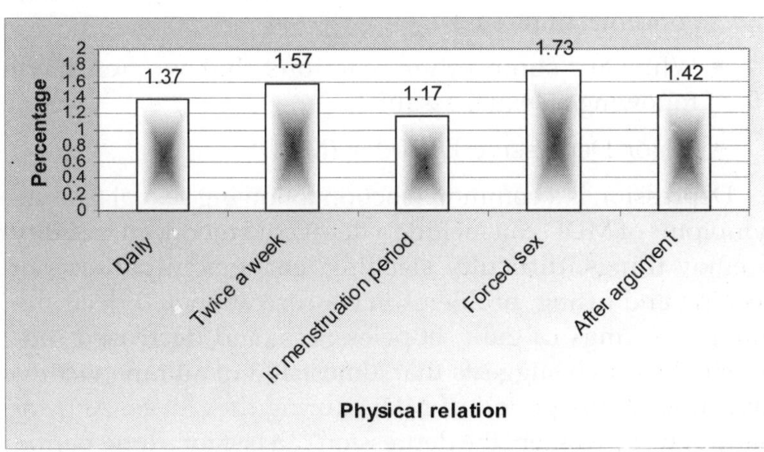

Fig. 5.12 : Impact of physical relation on women

difficulty concentrating and sleeping, and they may feel jumpy or on edge. While these initial reactions are normal and expected, some women may experience severe, highly disruptive symptoms that make it incredibly difficult to function in the first month following the assault. When these problems disrupt the woman's daily life, and prevent her from seeking assistance or telling friends and family members, the woman may have Acute Stress Disorder (ASD). Symptoms of ASD include :

- Feeling numb and detached, like being in a daze or a dream, or feeling that the world is strange and unreal.
- Difficulty remembering important parts of the assault.
- Reliving the assault through repeated thoughts, memories, or nightmares
- Avoidance of things (places, thoughts, feelings) that remind the woman of the assault
- Anxiety or increased arousal (e.g. difficulty sleeping, concentration, etc.)
- What are some other reactions that women have following a sexual assault?
- Major Depressive Disorder (MDD)

Depression is a common reaction following sexual assault. Symptoms of MDD can include a depressed mood, an inability to enjoy things, difficulty sleeping, changes in patterns of sleeping and eating, problems in concentration and decision-making, feelings of guilt, hopelessness, and decreased self-esteem. Research suggests that almost 1/3 of all rape victims have at least one period of MDD during their lives. And for many of these women, the depression can last for a long period of time. Thoughts about suicide are also common. Studies estimate that 1/3 of women who are raped contemplate suicide, and 17 per cent of rape victims actually attempt suicide.

Anger

Many victims of sexual assault report struggling with anger after the assault. Although this is a natural reaction to such a violating event, there is some research that suggests that prolonged, intense anger can interfere with the recovery process and further disrupt a woman's life.

Shame and Guilt

These feelings are common reactions to sexual assault. Some women blame themselves for what has happened or feel shameful about being an assault victim. This reaction can be even stronger among women who are assaulted by someone that they know, or who do not receive support from their friends, family, or authorities, following the incident. Shame and guilt can also get in a way of a woman's recovery by preventing her from telling others about what happened and getting assistance.

Social Problems

Social problems can sometimes arise following a sexual assault. A woman can experience problems in her marital relationship or in her friendships. Sometimes an assault survivor will be too anxious or depressed to want to participate in social activities. Many women report difficulty trusting others after the assault, so it can be difficult to develop new relationship. Performance at work and school can also be affected.

Sexual Problems

Sexual problems can be among the most long-standing problems experienced by women who are the victims of sexual assault. Women can be afraid of and try to avoid any sexual activity; they may experience an overall decrease in sexual interest and desire.

Alcohol and Drug Use

Substance abuse can sometimes become problematic for women who are the victims of assault. A large-scale study found that compared to non-victims, rape survivors were 3.4 times more likely to use marijuana, 6 times more likely to use cocaine, and 10 times more likely to use other major drugs. Often, women will report that they use these substances to control other symptoms related to their assault.

Table 5.13 : Impact of physical relation on women

Physical relation	Yes	No	Scores	Rank
Daily	90 (37.5)	150 (62.5)	1.37	IV
Twice a week	138 (57.5)	102 (42.5)	1.57	II
In menstruation period	42 (17.5)	198 (82.5)	1.17	V
Forcedly sex	175 (72.9)	65 (27.1)	1.73	I
After argument	101 (42.1)	139 (54.9)	1.42	III

Table 5.13 reveals that distribution of women respondents according to physical relation, 57.5 per cent women have made physical relation twice a week whereas 37.5 per cent women respondents have made relations daily. 17.5 per cent women respondents have made physical relations in menstruation period. In physical relations women have bound with their partner while her opinion yes or no it is not a question but her partner forcedly made a relation in menstruation period or daily like a sex violence. 72.9 per cent women respondents have made by physical relation forcedly whereas 42.1 per cent women have made after argument by her partner in the bed but it is a type II forcedly relation. Forcedly sex by partner is an act of aggression and violence women whose partners abuse them physically and sexually are at a higher risk of being seriously injured and killed. The assumption is that, once a woman enters into contract of marriage, the husband has the right to unlimited sexual access to his wife. 72.9 per cent women respondents replied that they have to undergo forced sex. 57.2 per cent made physical relations twice in a

week. Husbands feels it birth right to have physical relations after getting marriage. He ignores wife's emotions, acceptability or even her health. This is due to the ego of Indian males, through which he used to go for forced sex by all means.

Table 5.14 : Distribution of women as per seek first aid

First aid	Yes	No	Scores	Rank
At home	145 (60.4)	95 (39.6)	1.60	I
A medical clinic	84 (35.0)	156 (65.0)	1.35	II
Hospital emergency	32 (13.3)	208 (86.7)	1.13	III

Table 5.14 indicates first aid for an injury of women respondents, 60.4 women have taking first aid at home while 35.0 per cent women were taking first aid in medical clinic at injury. 13.3 per cent women respondents have hospitalized in emergency during major injury. Women whose partner abuse them physically and sexually are at a higher risk of being seriously injured and killed.

Table 5.15 : Promoting factors of domestic violence

Promoting factors	Yes	No	Scores	Rank
Family	100 (41.7)	140 (58.3)	1.42	III
Beauty	134 (55.8)	106 (44.2)	1.56	II
High economic status	64 (26.7)	176 (73.3)	1.27	VI
Extra marital relation	78 (32.5)	162 (67.5)	1.32	V
Friends	156 (65.0)	84 (35.0)	1.65	I
Restriction on talk with other males	87 (36.2)	153 (63.8)	1.36	IV

Table 5.15 shows that promoting factors of domestic violence, 65.0 per cent respondents have faced violence due to interaction of friends in personal matters whereas 55.8 per cent respondents have faced violence due to her beauty. 41.7 per cent respondents were faced domestic violence due to family by the in-laws. 32.5 per cent respondents were engaged

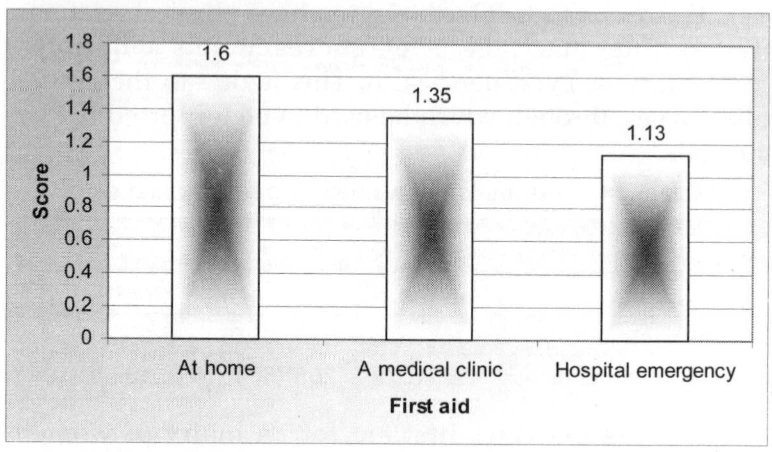

Fig. 5.13 : Distribution of women as per seek first aid

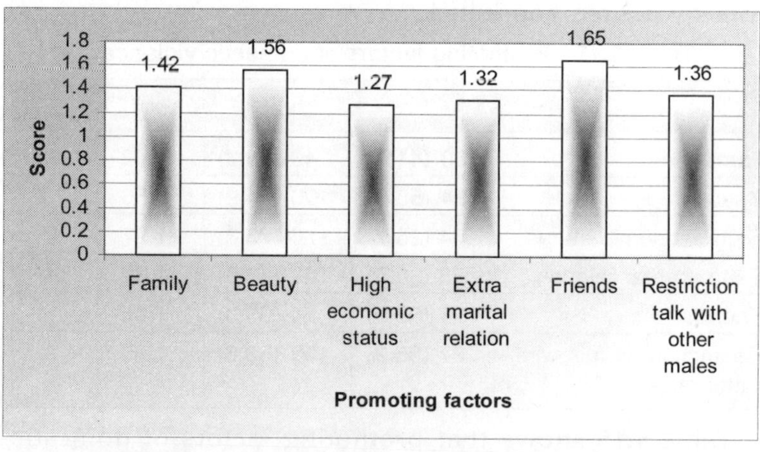

Fig. 5.14 : Promoting factors of domestic violence

in extra-marital relationship that is one of the factors of domestic violence. 36.2 per cent respondents were restricted to talk with other males, which gives rise to domestic violence in family.

The abuser is always responsible for the violence, and should be held accountable. There is not excuse for domestic violence and the victim is never responsible for the abuser's behaviour.

'Blame the victim' is something that abusers will often do to make excuses for their behaviour, and quite often they manage to convince their victims that the abuse is indeed their fault. This is part of the pattern and is in itself abusive. Blaming their behaviour on someone else, or on the relationship, their childhood, their ill health, or their alcohol or drug addiction is one way in which many abusers try to avoid personal responsibility for their behaviour.

It is important that any intervention to address domestic violence prioritises the safety of victims/survivors and holds the perpetrators accountable.

The terms 'victim' and 'survivor' are both used, depending on the context. 'Survivor' is, however, preferred as it emphasises an active, resourceful and creative response to the abuse, in contrast to 'victim', which implies passive acceptance. If you are reading this, then you are at least to some extent—a survivor.

Health Relationship : A connection between people that increases well-being, is mutually, enjoyable, and enhances or maintains each individual's positive self-concept. Health relationships are frequently characterized by good communication, trust, respect, honesty, equality, compromise, individuality, mutually fair problem solving, understanding/ empathy, self-confidence, mutual support. Healthy sexuality that one experiences sexuality in a state of physical, emotional, social and cultural well-being. It also means having the capacity to enjoy and control one's own sexual and reproductive behaviour in accordance with personal and social ethics, and is demonstrated by voluntary and responsible sexual expression that enrich individuals and their social lives. Lead to better understandings and experiences of our own sexualities and intimate relationships. Ensuring accountability and expectations of people to interact respectfully is a fundamental part of life.

Culture equitably values and relies on experiences and leadership from all members of society, including persons belonging to any historically oppressed group that has experienced systemic restrictions on their rights. Diverse people are engaged within their communities in activities promoting healthy relationships and healthy sexuality. Many promoting factors have been identified supporting domestic violence, 65 per cent women respondents replied that their counterparts became cruel due to provoking by their friends, 55.8 per cent respondents admits that being beautiful also creates complexes among males, due to which he suspects her and starts threatening. 32.5 per cent respondents admits the cruel behaviour arises due to extra marital relations, because husbands feels that he is not been able to do justice with his family and in overcoming this complex he starts violence.

Table 5.16 : Knowledge of respondents according to economic factors

Economic factors	Yes	No	Scores	Rank
Economic dependence	172 (71.7)	68 (28.3)	1.72	I
Limited access to cash and credit	126 (52.5)	114 (47.5)	1.52	II
Discriminatory laws	65 (27.1)	175 (72.9)	1.27	IV
Limited employment in sectors	54 (22.5)	186 (77.5)	1.22	V
Limited access to education and training	107 (44.6)	133 (55.4)	1.45	III

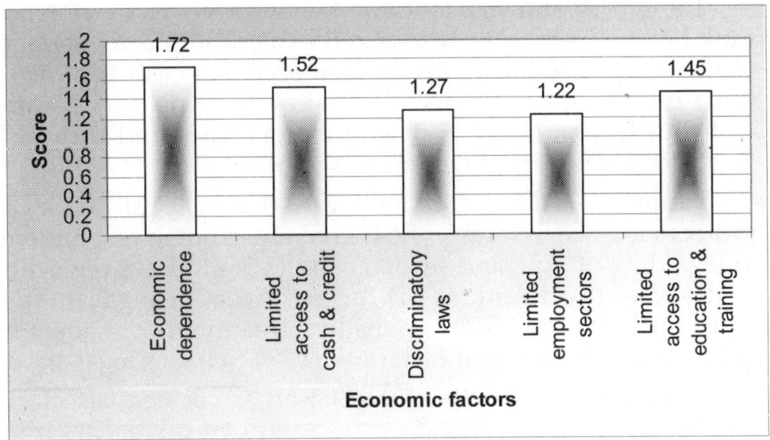

Fig. 5.15 : Knowledge of respondents according to economic factors

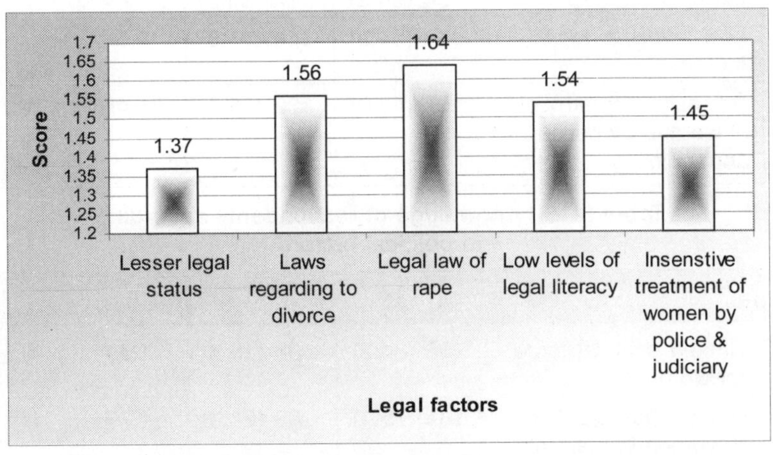

Fig. 5.16 : Knowledge of repondents as per legal factors

Table 5.16 shows economic factors involve in violence, rank I given by women respondents to economic dependence (1.72), second rank (1.52) to limited access to cash and credit, third rank (1.45) to limited access to education and training and fourth rank (1.27) to discriminatory laws and fifth rank (1.22) to limited employment in sectors.

Table 5.17 shows *(See on page 84)* that legal factors to protect violence first rank (1.64) given by women respondents to legal law of rape and second rank (1.56) to laws regarding to divorce, third rank (1.54) to low levels of legal literacy and fourth rank (1.45) to insensitive treatment of women by police and judiciary and fifth rank (1.37) to lesser legal status.

Table 5.17 : Knowledge of respondents as per legal factors

Legal factors	Yes	No	Scores	Rank
Lesser legal status	88 (36.7)	152 (63.3)	1.37	V
Laws regarding to divorce	134 (55.8)	106 (44.2)	1.56	II
Legal law of rape	154 (64.2)	86 (35.8)	1.64	I
Low levels of legal literacy	130 (54.2)	110 (45.8)	1.54	III
Insensitive treatment of women by police and judiciary	108 (45.0)	132 (55.0)	1.45	IV

Table 5.18 : Knowledge of respondents according to political factors

Political factors	Yes	No	Scores	Rank
Limited political force for women	202 (84.2)	38 (15.8)	1.84	II
Limited participation of women in political system	181 (75.4)	59 (24.6)	1.75	III
Risk of challenge to religious laws	162 (67.5)	78 (32.5)	1.68	IV
Violence not taken seriously	209 (87.1)	31 (12.9)	1.87	I

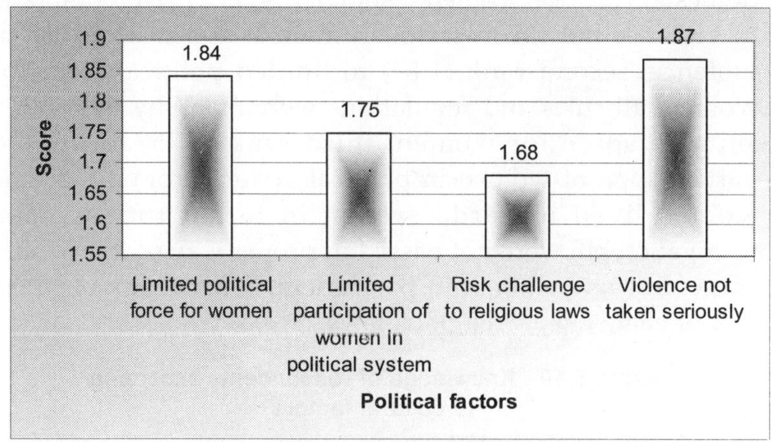

Fig. 5.17 : Knowledge of respondents according to political factors

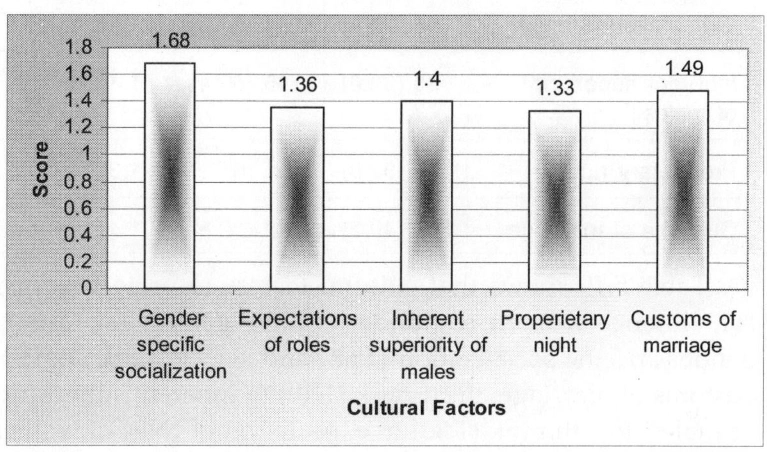

Fig. 5.18 : Knowledge of respondents according to cultural factors

Table 5.18 shows that political factors responsible for domestic violence, women respondents (1.87) given first rank to violence not taken seriously then it is a main cause of violence, second rank (1.84) to limited political force for women, all rules and regulations were made by men not a suitable space for women, third rank (1.75) to limited participation of women in political system, from a old time women lived in parda system in recent time women reservation bill were not passed in proper way so it is a main cause and few women in parliament, fourth rank (1.68) to risk of challenge to religious laws.

Table 5.19 : Knowledge of respondents according to cultural factors

Cultural factors	Yes	No	Scores	Rank
Gender specific socialization	162 (67.5)	78 (32.5)	1.68	I
Expectation of roles	86 (35.8)	154 (64.2)	1.36	IV
Inherent superiority of males	95 (39.6)	145 (60.4)	1.40	III
Proprietary right	79 (32.9)	161 (67.1)	1.33	V
Customs of marriage	118 (49.2)	122 (50.8)	1.49	II

Table 5.19 shows that cultural factors to protect women for violence women respondents have given first rank to gender specific socialization (1.68) and second rank (1.49) to customs of marriage, third rank (1.40) to inherent superiority of males, fourth rank (1.36) to expectation of roles of women and others and gives last rank to proprietary rights. Investigations by human rights watch have found that is cases of domestic violence, law enforcement officials frequently reinforce the batterer's attempts to control and demean their victims.

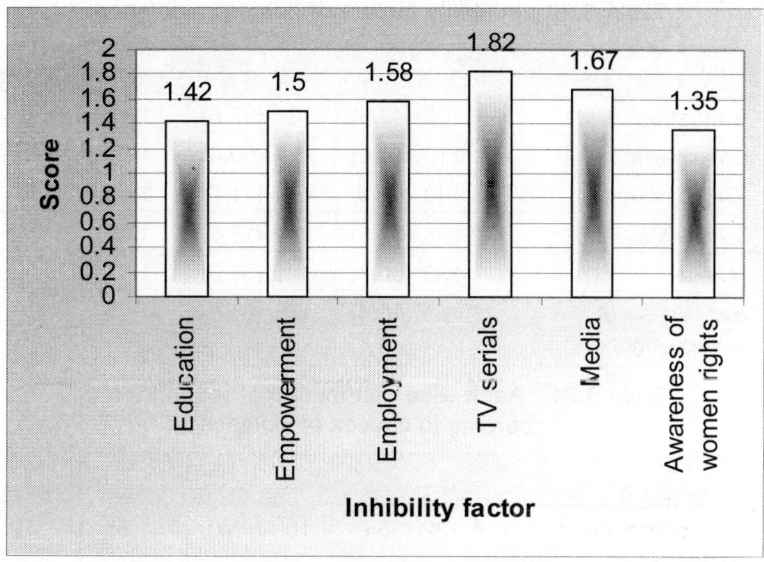

Fig. 5.19 : Inhibility factors of domestic violence

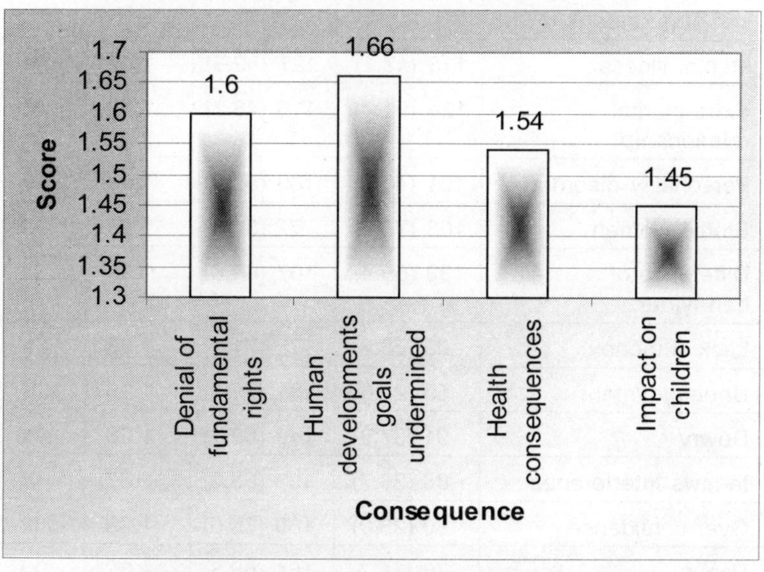

Fig. 5.20 : Opinion of respondents according to consequences about violence

Table 5.20 : Inhibility factors of domestic violence

Cultural factors	Yes	No	Scores	Rank
Education	102 (42.5)	138 (57.5)	1.42	V
Empowerment	119 (49.6)	121 (50.4)	1.50	IV
Employment	140 (58.3)	100 (41.7)	1.58	III
TV serials	198 (82.5)	42 (17.5)	1.82	I
Media	160 (66.7)	80 (33.3)	1.67	II
Awareness of women rights	85 (35.4)	155 (64.6)	1.35	IV

Table 5.21 : Rank-wise distribution of respondents according to causes of violence

Causes	Yes	No	Scores	Rank
Age difference of partner	132 (55.0)	108 (45.0)	1.55	IV
Difference of education of partner	149 (62.1)	91 (37.9)	1.62	II
Mental illness	113 (47.1)	127 (52.9)	1.47	VI
Extra-marital relationship	124 (51.7)	116 (48.3)	1.52	V
Personality disorder	101 (42.1)	139 (57.9)	1.42	VII
Sterile women	168 (70.0)	72 (30.0)	1.70	I
Difference of behaviour	133 (55.4)	107 (44.6)	1.55	III
Lack of money	68 (28.3)	172 (71.7)	1.28	XII
Unemployment	59 (24.6)	181 (75.4)	1.25	XIV
Dowry	91 (37.9)	149 (62.1)	1.38	VIII
In-laws interference	88 (36.7)	152 (63.3)	1.37	IX
Over confidence	60 (25.0)	180 (75.0)	1.25	XIII
Beauty	76 (31.7)	164 (68.3)	1.32	XI
Frustration	82 (34.2)	158 (65.8)	1.34	X

Table 5.20 reveals that women respondents were aware about inhibility factors, first rank to TV serials 82.5 per cent respondents were see serials in TV to aware about violence whereas 66.7 per cent women were protect about media factor. 58.3 per cent women were safe due to employment and earned money for the family whereas, 49.6 per cent respondents were empowerment due to nature and various causes. 42.5 per cent women were taking education and 35.4 per cent women aware of women rights.

Stress may be increased when a person is living in a family situation, with increased pressures. Social stresses, due to inadequate finances or other such problems in a family may further increase tensions. Violence is not always caused by stress, but may be one way that some people respond to stress. Families and couples in poverty may be more likely to experience domestic violence, due to increased stress and conflicts about finances and other aspects. Some speculate that poverty may hinder a man's ability to live up to his idea of 'successful manhood', thus he fears losing honour and respect. Theory suggests that when he is unable to economically support his wife, and maintain control, he may turn to misogyny, substance abuse, and crime as ways to express masculinity. 82.5 per cent women replied that they have become aware by viewing television serials and keep an eye on their counterparts. 66.7 per cent women replied that violence is commonly seen in extra marital relations in media. Domestic violence can be prevented by sting operations.

Table 5.21 reveals that rank distribution of respondents according to causes of violence, 70.0 per cent women respondents have sterile women for arises of domestic violence whereas 62.1 per cent respondents were faced difference of education of partner causes difference between couple. 55.0 per cent respondents causes violence due to age difference of partner whereas 51.7 per cent women were engaged extra marital relationship. 55.4 per cent respondents have difference of behaviour of the partner whereas 47.1 per cent respondents were faced mental illness to be the cause of violence. 37.9 per cent women respondents were faced violence due to dowry, whereas 36.7 per cent women were faced in-laws interference in personal life. 25.0 per cent women were faced causes of violence due to over confidence and 51.66 per cent due to beauty. 34.2 per cent women respondents were suffering from frustration in daily life causes violence whereas 28.3 per cent women have lack of money causes of violence. 24.6 per cent respondents were unemployment due to causes of violence.

Table 5.22 : Opinion of the respondents according to consequences about violence

Consequences	Yes	No	Scores	Rank
Denial of fundamental rights	143 (59.6)	97 (40.4)	1.60	II
Human development goals undermined	158 (65.8)	82 (34.2)	1.66	I
Health consequences	130 (54.2)	110 (45.8)	1.54	III
Impact on children	108 (45.0)	132 (55.0)	1.45	IV

Table 5.22 indicates that consequences of women respondents in violence, women given to first rank (1.66) to human development goals undermined in full potential as long as women's potential to participate fully in their society is denied. Social, economic and health costs of violence leave the violence against women undermines and economic development, second rank given by women (1.60) to denial of fundamental rights most crucial consequences of violence against women and girls, international human rights instruments such as the Universal Declaration of Human Rights (UDHR) in 1948 and the Convention on the Rights of the Child (CRC) in 1989). Third rank (1.54) given by women respondents to health consequences like physical and psychological consequences, some with fatal outcomes.

The impact of violence on women's mental health leads to severe and fatal consequences. Health consequences of violence against women in physical health outcomes are injury, unwanted pregnancy, miscarriage, pelvic inflammatory disease, chronic pelvic pain, asthma, headaches, irritable bowel syndrome and self-injurious (smoking, unprotected sex). Mental health outcomes like depression, fear, anxiety and post traumatic stress disorder and fatal outcomes like suicide, maternal mortality and HIV. Fourth rank (1.45) to impact on children who have witnessed domestic violence or have themselves been abused, exhibit health and behaviour problems. They may try to run away or even display suicidal tendencies.

There are varied consequences of domestic violence depending on the victim, the age group, the intensity of the violence and frequency of the torment they are subjected to. Living under a constant fear, threat and humiliation are some of the feelings developed in the minds of the victims as a consequence of an atrocious violence. The consequences of the domestic violence in detail can be broadly categorised under—the effect on the victim himself/herself and the family, effect on the society and the effect on nation's growth and productivity. The 'Effect on the victim' has been under subcategorised for women, men children and olds.

Battered women have tendency to remain quiet, agonized and emotionally disturbed after the occurrence of the torment. A psychological set back and trauma because of domestic violence affects women's productivity in all forms of life. The suicide case of such victimized women is also a deadly consequence and the number of such cases is increasing.

A working Indian woman may drop out from work place because of the ill-treatment at home or office, she may lose her inefficiency in work. Her health may deteriorate if she is not well physically and mentally. Some women leave their home immediately after first few atrocious attacks and try to become self-dependent. Their survival becomes difficult and painful when they have to work hard for earning two meals a day. Many such women come under rescue of women welfare organizations like Women Welfare Association of India (WWAI), Affus Woman Welfare Association (AWWA) and Woman's Emancipation and Development Trust (WEDT). Some of them who leave their homes are forcefully involved in women trafficking and pornography. This results in acquiring a higher risk of becoming a drug addict and suffering from HIV/AIDS. Some of course do it by their choice.

One of the severe effects of domestic violence against women is its effect on her children. It is nature's phenomenon that a child generally has a greater attachment towards the mother for she is the one who gives birth. As long as the violence subjected to the mother is hidden from the child, he/she may behave normally at home. The day when mother's grief and suffering is revealed, a child may become upset about the happening deeply. Children may not even comprehend the severity of the problem. They may turn silent, reserved and express solace to the mother. When the violence against women is openly done in front of them since their childhood, it may have a deeper and gruesome impact in their mindset. They get used to such happenings at home, and have a tendency to reciprocate the same in their lives. It's common in especially in rural homes in India which are victimized by the evil of domestic violence.

In case of Intimate Partner Violence (IPV), violence against women leads them to maintain a distance from their partner. Their sexual life is affected adversely. Many of them file for divorce and seek separation which again affects the life of children. Some continue to be exploited in lack of proper awareness of human rights and laws of the constitution.

All the different forms of violence discussed in this essay adversely affect the society. Violence against women may keep them locked in homes succumbing to the torture they face. If they come out in open and reveal the wrong done to them for help and rescue, it influences the society both positively and negatively. At one hand where it acts as an inspiration and ray of hope for other suffering women, on the other hand it also spoils the atmosphere of the society. When something of this kind happens in the society, few families may witness the evil of domestic violence knocking their door steps. Some families try to imitate what others indulge in irrespective of it being good or bad for the family.

Violence against women includes intimate partner violence, sexual violence, and other forms of violence against women committed by acquaintances or strangers. Victims of violence can experience physical injury; mental health consequences such as depression, anxiety, low self-esteem and suicide attempts; and other health consequences such as gastrointestinal disorders, substance abuse, sexually transmitted diseases, and gynaecological or pregnancy complications. These consequences can lead to hospitalization, disability, or death.

Intimate partner violence is actual or threatened physical, sexual, psychological, or emotional abuse by a current or former spouse (including common-law spouse), dating partner, or boyfriend or girlfriend. Intimate partners can be of the same or opposite sex. Women experience more chronic and injurious assaults from intimate partner violence than men.

Sexual violence is a completed or attempted sex act against the victim's will or involving a victim who is unable to consent; abusive sexual contact; and non-contact sexual abuse, including sexual harassment. It is committed by an intimate or non-intimate perpetrator such as a spouse, family member, friend, person in position of power or trust, acquaintance, or stranger. Although there is some overlap between intimate partner violence and sexual violence, the latter is committed by a wider range of perpetrators.

Perhaps the most crucial consequence of violence against women and girls is the denial of fundamental human rights to women and girls. International human rights instruments such as the Universal Declaration of Human Rights (UDHR), adopted in 1948, the Convention on the Elimination of All Forms of Discrimination Against Women (CEDAW), adopted in 1979, and the Convention on the Rights of the Child (CRC), adopted in 1989, affirm the principles of fundamental rights and freedoms of every human being. Both CEDAW and the CRC are guided by a broad concept of human rights that stretches beyond civil and political rights to the core issues of economic survival, health, and education that affect the quality of daily life for most women and children. The two conventions call for the right to protection from gender-based abuse and neglect.

The strength of these treaties rests on an international consensus, and the assumption that all practices that harm women and girls, no matter how deeply they are embedded in culture, must be eradicated. Legally binding under international law for governments that have ratified them, these treaties oblige governments not only to protect women from crimes of violence, but also to investigate violations when they occur and to bring the perpetrators to justice.

There is a growing recognition that countries cannot reach their full potential as long as women's potential to participate fully in their society is denied. Data on the social, economic and health costs of violence leave no doubt that violence against women undermines progress towards human and economic development. Women's participation has become key in all social development programmes, environmental, for poverty alleviation, or for good governance. By hampering the full involvement and participation of women, countries are eroding the human capital of half their populations. True indicators of a country's commitment to gender equality lie in its actions to eliminate violence against women in all its forms and in all areas of life.

Domestic violence against women leads to far-reaching physical consequences, some with fatal outcomes. While physical injury represents only a part of the negative health impacts on women, it is among the more visible forms of violence. The United States Department of Justice has reported that 37 per cent of all women who sought medical care in hospital emergence rooms for violence-related injuries were injured by a current or former spouse or partner. Assaults result in injuries ranging from business and fractures to chronic disabilities such as partial or total loss of hearing or vision, and burns may lead to disfigurement. The medical complications resulting from FGM can range from haemorrhage and sterility to severe psychological trauma. Studies in many countries have shown high levels of violence during pregnancy resulting in risk to the health of both the mother and the unborn foetus. In the worst cases, all of these examples of domestic violence can result in the death of the woman—murdered by her current or ex-partner.

Sexual assaults and rape can lead to unwanted pregnancies, and the dangerous complications that follow from resorting to illegal abortions. Girls who have been sexually abused in their childhood are more likely to engage in risky behaviour such as early sexual intercourse, and are at greater risk of unwanted and early pregnancies. Women in violence situations are less able to use contraception or negotiate safer sex, and therefore run a high risk of contracting sexually transmitted diseases and HIV/AIDS.

The impact of violence on women's mental health leads to severe and fatal consequences. Battered women have a high incidence of stress and stress-related illnesses such as post-traumatic stress syndrome, panic attacks, depression, sleeping and eating disturbances, elevated blood pressure, alcoholism, drug abuse, and low self-esteem. For some women, fatally depressed and demeaned by their abuser, there seems to be no escape from a violent relationship except suicide.

Health consequences can result directly from violent acts or from the long-term effects of violence.

- **Injuries :** Physical and sexual abuse by a partner is closely associated with injuries. Violence by an intimate partner is the leading cause of non-fatal injuries to women in the USA.
- **Death :** Deaths from violence against women include honour killings (by families for cultural reasons); suicide; female infanticide (murder of infant girls); and maternal death from unsafe abortion.
- **Sexual and reproductive health :** Violence against women is associated with sexually transmitted infections such as HIV/AIDS, unintended pregnancies, gynaecological problems, induced abortions, and adverse pregnancy outcomes, including miscarriage, low birth weight and fetal death.
- **Risky behaviour :** Sexual abuse as a child is associated with higher rates of sexual risk-taking (such as first sex at an early age, multiple partners and unprotected sex), substance use, and additional victimization. Each of these behaviours increases risks of health problems.

Power and Control Wheel

- **Mental health :** Violence and abuse increase risk of depression, post-traumatic stress disorder, sleep difficulties, eating disorders and emotional distress.

Table 5.23 : Distribution of women respondents according to power and control by their partner

Power and control	Frequency	Per Cent
Dominance	48	20.0
Humiliation	64	26.7
Isolation	58	24.2
Threats	38	15.8
Intimidation	23	9.6
Denial and blame	9	3.7
Total	**240**	**100.0**

- **Physical health :** Abuse can result in many health problems, including headaches, back pain, abdominal pain, fibromyalgia, gastrointestinal disorders, limited mobility, and poor overall health.

Table 5.23 reveals that power and control steps used by abusers to get and keep control in their relationship. Abusive individuals need to feel in charge of the relationship, 26.7 per cent respondents have controlled humiliation then believe worthless and that no one else will want less likely to leave. 20.0 per cent abusers used dominance. The abuser need to feel in-charge of the relationship. 24.2 per cent women have isolation in order to increase dependence on him an abusive partner will cut off from the outside world. 15.8 per cent women have threats to keep their victims from leaving or to scare them into dropping charges. 9.6 per cent women were intimidation tactics designed to scare into submission, include making threatening looks or gestures, smashing things in front of destroying property, hurting or putting weapons on display 3.7 per cent women were denial and blame their abusive and

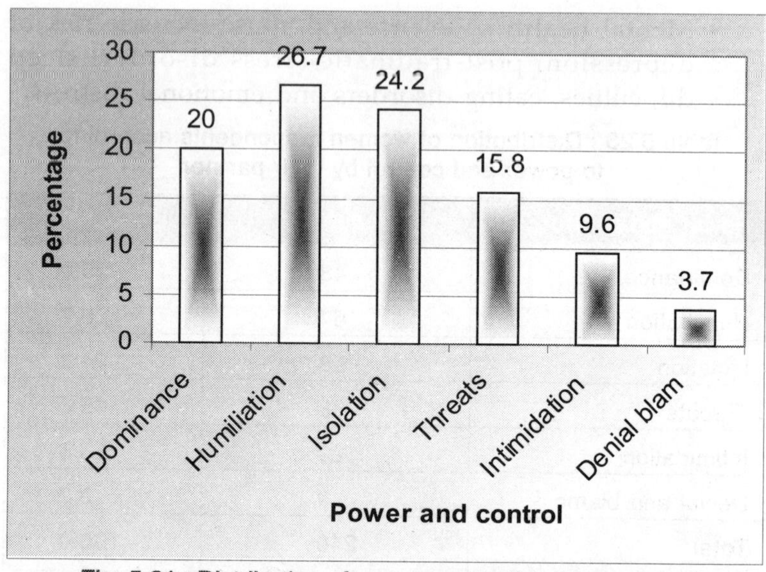

Fig. 5.21 : Distribution of women according to power and control by their partner

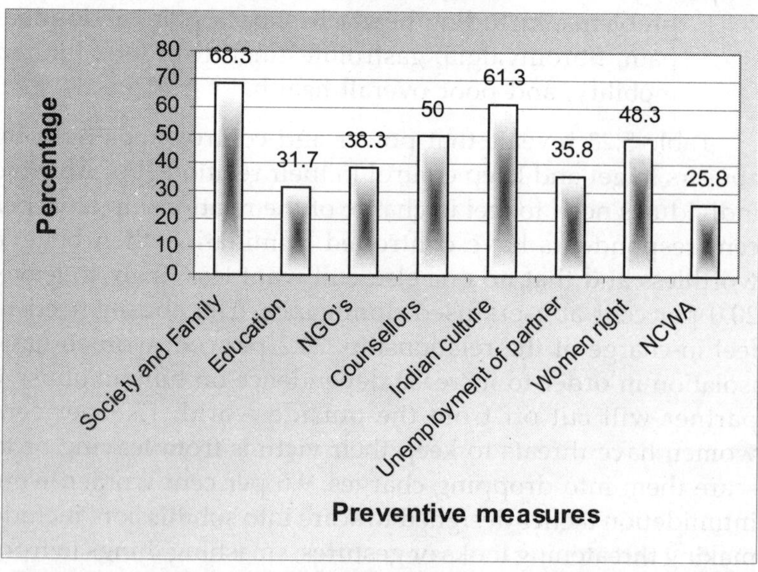

Fig. 5.22 : Distribution of respondents according to preventive measures of violence

violent behaviour on a bad childhood and even on the victims of their abuse.

A wide range of effects from domestic violence. The perpetrator's abusive behaviour can cause an array of health problems and physical injuries. Victimes may require medical attention for immediate injuries, hospitalization for severe assaults, or chronic care for debilitating health problems resulting from the perpetrator's physical attacks. The direct physical effects of domestic violence can range from minor scratches or bruises to fractured bones or sexually transmitted diseases resulting from forced sexual activity and other practices. The indirect physical effects of domestic violence can range from recurring headaches or stomachaches to severe health problems due to withheld medical attention or medications.

Many victims of abuse make frequent visits to their physicians for health problems and for domestic violence-related injuries. Unfortunately, research shows that many victims will not disclose the abuse unless they are directly asked or screened for domestic violence by the physician. It is imperative, therefore, that health care providers directly inquire about possible domestic violence so victims receive proper treatment for injuries or illnesses and are offered further assistance for addressing the abuse.

The impact of domestic violence on victims can result in acute and chronic mental health problems. Some victims, however, have histories of psychiatric illnesses that may be exacerbated by the abuse; others may develop psychological problems as a direct result of the abuse. Examples of emotional and behavioural effects of domestic violence include many common coping responses to trauma, such as :

- Emotional withdrawal
- Denial or minimization of the abuse
- Impulsivity or aggressiveness
- Apprehension or fear
- Helplessness

- Anger
- Anxiety or hyper vigilance
- Disturbance of eating or sleeping patterns
- Substance abuse
- Depression
- Suicide
- Post-traumatic stress disorder

Some of these effects also serve as coping mechanisms for victims. For example, some victims turn to alcohol to lessen the physical and emotional pain of the abuse. Unfortunately, these coping mechanisms can serve as barriers for victims who want help or want to leave their abusive relationships. Psychiatrists, psychologists, therapists, and counselors who provide screening, comprehensive assessment, and treatment for victims can serve as the catalyst that helps them address or escape the abuse.

Table 5.24 : Distribution of respondents according to preventive measures of violence

Preventive measures	Frequency	Per Cent
Society and family	164	68.3
Education	76	31.7
NGO's	92	38.3
Counsellor's	122	50.8
Indian culture	147	61.3
Unemployment of partner	86	35.8
Women rights	116	48.3
NCWA	62	25.8

Table 5.24 shows that 68.3 per cent women have safe about society and family to preventive measures of violence whereas 61.3 per cent women were faced preventive factors of Indian culture. 50.8 per cent women were used to advice of counsellor's whereas 48.3 per cent respondents were used

women rights for preventive measures of violence. 38.3 per cent women were taking advice for NGO's to prevent violence.

Further evaluation is needed to assess the effectiveness of violence prevention measures. Interventions with promising results include increasing education and opportunities for women and girls, improving their self-esteem and negotiating skills, and reducing gender inequities in communities.

Other efforts with positive outcomes include : work with teenagers to reduce dating violence; programmes that support children who have witnessed intimate partner violence; mass public education campaigns; and work with men and boys to change attitudes towards gender inequities and the acceptability of violence.

Advocacy for victims, better awareness of violence and its consequences among health workers, and wider knowledge of available resources for abused women (including legal assistance, housing and child care), can lessen the consequences of violence.

Preventing violence against women requires the support and contributions of many patterns; federal agencies, state and local health departments, non-profit organizations, academic institutions, international agencies, and private industry. Partners help in a variety of ways, including collecting data about violence, learning about risk factors, developing strategies for prevention, and ensuring that effective prevention approaches reach those in need.

The National Sexual Violence Resource Center (NSVRC) identifies and disseminates information, resources, and research on all aspects of sexual violence prevention and intervention. Staff provide customized technical assistance, collaborate with other national and local organizations, and specialize in offering resources for underserved communities. Additional activities include coordinating national sexual assault awareness activities; identifying emerging policy issues and research needs; issuing a biannual newsletter, and recommending speakers and trainers. The NSVRC website features links to resources, including information about conferences, funding, jobs, research, and special events. The Center serves state sexual assault coalitions, rape crisis centers, government agencies, U.S. Territories and tribal entities, colleges and universities, service providers, researchers, allied organizations, policymakers, media, and the public.

CDC is funding the University of North Carolina Injury Prevention Research Center to develop a national training programme for violence prevention practitioners. Preventing Violence through Education, Networking and Technical Assistance (PREVENT) works with individuals and organizations to build skills in identifying community needs and assets, creating and mobilizing partnerships, developing and implementing prevention programmes, measuring success, and funding and sustaining programmes.

The National Online Resource Center on Violence Against Women (VAWnet) provides support for the development, implementation, and maintenance of effective violence against women intervention and prevention efforts at national, state, and local levels. VAWnet provides a collection of full-text, searchable electronic resources on domestic violence, sexual violence and related issues to state domestic violence and sexual assault coalition, allied organizations, and the public. It offers useful links; monitors news coverage of violence against women issues; provides calendars of trainings, conferences and grant deadlines; and presents information about Domestic Violence Awareness and Sexual Assault Awareness Months.

Prevention Connection : The Violence Against Women Prevention Partnership features a listserv and bi-monthly, web-based forums designed to build the capacity of local, state, national and tribal agencies and organizations to develop, implement, and evaluate effective violence against women prevention initiatives. The Prevent-Connect Listserv provides a vehicle for ongoing analysis and discussion of domestic and sexual violence prevention efforts. The forums feature a variety of prevention experts who explore and discuss approaches and comprehensive solutions to domestic and sexual violence. Prevention Connection is a project of the California Coalition Against Sexual Assault.

CDC has developed a guide for violence against women programmes to provide practitioners with information about how to conduct evaluations based on strong scientific methods. The guide will assist programmes in identifying measurable objectives and goals and in linking these objectives and goals with services and evaluation plans. Information about data collection methodology and measures, data analyses, presentation of results, and selection of an external evaluator are included. The guide will be published in late 2005.

Table 5.25 : Correlation coefficient between domestic violence and variables

Variables	'r'
Age	0.4132*
Education	0.3885*
Caste	0.3661*
Religion	0.4672*
Income	0.4185*

The perusal of Table 5.25 reveals that correlation coefficient between domestic violence and variables, age (0.4132*), education (0.3885*), caste (0.3661*), religion (0.4672*) and income (0.4185*) significantly correlated with domestic violence like physical abuse, sexual abuse, emotional abuse and economic abuse. Domestic violence is an abuse of power perpetrated mainly by men against women either in a relationship. The most commonly acknowledged forms are physical and sexual violence, threats and intimidation, emotional and social abuse and economic deprivation.

6

Summary and Conclusion

Women and children are often in great danger in the place where they should be safest; within their families. For many, 'home' is where they face a regime of terror and violence at the hands of somebody close to them—somebody they should be able to trust. Those victimized suffer physically and psychologically. They are unable to make their own decisions, voice their own opinions or protect themselves and their children for fear of further repercussions. Their human rights are denied and their lives are stolen from them by the ever-present threat of violence.

In recent years, there has been a greater understanding of the problem of domestic violence, its causes and consequences, and an international consensus has developed on the need to deal with the issue. The Convention on the Elimination of All Forms of Discrimination against Women adopted by the United Nations General Assembly some 20 years ago, the decade-old Convention on the Rights of the Child, and the Platform for Action adopted at the Fourth International Conference on Women in Beijing in 1995, all reflect this consensus. But progress has been slow because attitudes are deeply entrenched and, to some extent, because effective strategies to address domestic violence are still being defined. As a result, women worldwide continue to suffer, with estimates varying from 20 to 50 per cent from country to country.

While the impact of physical abuse may be more 'visible' than psychological scarring, repeated humiliation and insults, forced isolation, limitations on social mobility, constant threats of violence and injury, and denial of economic resources are more subtle and insidious forms of violence. The intangible nature of psychological abusc makes it harder to define and report, leaving the woman in a situation where she is often made to feel mentally destabilized and powerless.

Jurists and human rights experts and activities have argued that the physical, sexual and psychological abuse, sometimes with fatal outcomes, inflicted on women is comparable to torture in both its nature and severity. It can be perpetrated internationally, and committed for the specific purposes of punishment, intimidation, and control of the women's identity and behaviour. It takes place in situations where a woman may seem free to leave, but is held prisoner by fear of further violence against herself and her children, or by lack of resources, family, legal or community support.

Objectives

1. To study the socio-economic status of victim.
2. To ascertain the kinds of domestic violence in the study area.
3. To identify factors responsible for the domestic violence in the family.
4. To study the causes and consequences of violence on women.
5. To evaluate the practicability of preventive measures.

Research Methodology

The study was conducted in Lucknow district. Four zones were selected in this study area. Total 240 females were selected in this study area. Dependent and independent variables were used such as caste, age, education and violence, causes, preventive measures. The statistical tools were used such as χ^2, mean, cr.

Major Findings

1. Violence were slapping, kicking, tearing, hair pushing and pulling, hitting with an object, attempting to strangulate and threatening in 21 to 45 years age-group. Abuse of women is common in society and can happen to people regardless of their age, culture, religion, income or education. As per government rule the marriageable age of girls has been recommended as 21 years. So all the respondents selected in the study are in the age-group of 21-45 years. It is obvious that domestic violence are also found in this age group. However, in the present study, the highest 49.2 per cent cases of domestic violence have been found in the age group of 29-37 years. In this age group females after spending 5 to 10 years with their partner feel themselves as matured and claim for equal status with husband in the family. This results often in bad relations with partner in life.
2. Minimum 18.8 per cent women respondents have passed only Intermediate or illiterate. These women have managed to mobilize hundreds of other women, raised resources, designed strategies and forced policy makes to revise laws and policies. Women need to be empowered through education. There seems to be no effect of education on domestic violence, because in the modern scenario, even after being empowered and educated, girls do tolerate the husband's cruelties like

beating, addiction with alcohol, having extra-marital relations and fighting on even small issues due to the fear from the society that the domestic issues may become public. They do tolerate all these up to a limit. However, illiterate women behave just reverse. They do not have fear of society and never felt sorry in putting their problem of violence in front of others. Number of examples can be cited like the fearless exposing character of playback singer Udit Narain by first wife and cases of wives of many politicians etc.

3. Violence is a learned behaviour that is usually passed on from one generation to next, unless efforts are made to interrupt the dysfunctional pattern. Poverty, alcoholism and mental illness all are further risk factors, and violence against women also is shaped by class, sexuality and other social divisions. It has been seen in the study that most of the domestic violence has been found among lower caste families because both the partners are mostly illiterate and they do not have the fear of society. However, now-a-days domestic violence is increasing among middle class families too, due to professional tension, poor economic condition, high ambitiousness, lack of patience and extra marital relations.
4. Religion plays an important role in emotional or psychological abuse to chip away at feelings of self-worth and independence. Traditions respondents the beliefs, values and way of thinking of a social group. Tradition as a social custom passed down from one generation to another through the process of socialization. Every religion have thin own tradition and beliefs. Most of the domestic violence has been found in Hindu families due to religious and social restrictions. As per Islamic rules, 4 marriage are legal in Muslim families and business group dominates in

Muslim community. They do not posses qualities of high ambition, illiteracy rate is also very high.

5. Now-a-days joint family system disintegrate into nuclear family system. In urban areas joint family system convert into nuclear family system while in rural areas it become slow. Domestic violence are less in joint family system due to the fear of older persons and shyness. However, 10 per cent cases have been reported in such families where older ones are conservative, greedy and aggressive.
6. Domestic violence is very common among house wives and service women, because service women have to spent 50 per cent of her time towards service due to which she has to face threatening of her partner. Housewives also may not get the due importance, because of the husband's mentality, who recognize their wives to be meant for keeping his house, giving birth to children and to fulfill his sexual desire. Because of this mentality, nearly 50 per cent relationships become worse even in 10 years of marriage.
7. Violence against women is present in every country, cutting across boundaries of culture, class, education, income, ethnicity and age. The global dimensions of this violence are alarming, as highlighted by studies on its incidence and prevalence. The social and economic costs of violence against women are enormous and have ripple effects throughout society. Women may suffer isolation, inability to work, loss of wages, lack of participation in regular activities, and limited ability to care for themselves and their children. If cases where women earns more, Her husband fails to do much violence because, he consider her as a earning resource, which fulfills his family economic desires.
8. 17.9 per cent women have faced sexual abuse can involve excessive jealousy, calling sexually derogatory

names, criticizing and forcing unwanted sexual act, sadistic sexual acts, forcing sex after physical assault, taking unwanted sexual photos and forcing for sex when ill or tired. Domestic violence and abuse can happen to anyone, yet the problem is often overlooked, excused, or denied. This is especially true when the abuse is psychological, rather than physical. Emotional abuse is often minimized, yet it can leave deep and lasting scars.

Sexual harassment in the workplace is a growing concern for women. Employers abuse their authority to seek sexual favours from their female co-workers or subordinates, sometimes promising promotions or other forms of career advancement or simply creating an untenable and hostile work environment. Women who refuse to give into such unwanted sexual advances often run the risk of anything from demotion to dismissal. Most women initially victimized by sexual traffickers have little inkling of what awaits them. They generally get a very small percentage of what the customer pays to the pimp or the brothel owner. Once they are caught up in the system there is practically no way out, and they find themselves in a very vulnerable situation. Many women and girl children are trafficked across borders, often with the complicity of border guards. In one incident, five young prostitutes burned to death in a brothel fire because they had been chained to their beds. At the same time, sex tours of developing countries are a well-organized industry in several European and other industrialized countries.

9. There are many signs of an abusive relationship. The most telling sign is fear of partner. If you feel like you have to walk on eggshells around your partner-constantly watching what you say and do in order to avoid a blow-up—chances are your relationship is unhealthy and abusive. Other signs that you may be in

an abusive relationship include a partner who belittles you or tries to control you, and feelings of self-loathing, helplessness, and desperation.

10. 50.0 per cent male have taking Gutkha whereas, 34.2 per cent respondent's partner were taking alcohol. 5.8 per cent male were found to be addicted with Bhang, whereas, 16.7 per cent male have addicted to smoking like cigarette/bidi and 7.9 per cent males were found of taking drugs. 26.2 per cent male partner haves always suspicious about female sex and 17.1 per cent male partner have suffering form psyche. Although most researches focus on men as abusers of women, research also indicates that women abuse men about as often. And there's no reason to believe that alcohol causes women to abuse men. Husbands who are addicted with wine, drugs, cocaine or using cigarette or bidi, they get irritated early, become aggressive and loose patience easily. These acts hurts their wives. In the study, 26.2 per cent husbands are found to be mysterious, whose wives do not expect the kind of behaviour from their counterparts, 17.7 per cent husband were found psychic, who kept doubt and threat their wives. These actions put their wives always in a fearful environment.

11. 41.7 per cent women were remain silent during violence. They were taking all type of abuse and violence silently not given any objection and argue whereas, 16.7 per cent women protected herself during violence and various abuse. They were defended herself with their partner. 16.2 per cent women respondents have leave home after violence and abuses, they were choosing safe side but it is not a solution to stop the violence while 15.0 per cent women have taking defend side by argue to protect herself, some educated women were taking this type of reaction. 4.2 per cent respondents also reacted same during violence. In the early stages,

many women report feeling shock, confusion, anxiety, and/or numbness. Sometimes women will experience feelings of denial. In other words, they may not fully acknowledge what has happened to them or they may downplay the intensity of the experience. This reaction may be more common among women are assaulted by someone they know.

12. 17.5 per cent women respondents have made physical relations in menstruation period. In physical relations women are bound with their partner irrespect of her opinion yes or no it is not a question but her partner forcedly made a relations in menstruation period or daily like a sex violence. Forced sex by partner is an act of aggression and violence with women whose partners abuse them physically and sexually are at a higher risk of being seriously injured and killed. The assumption is that, once a woman enters into contract of marriage, the husband has the right to unlimited sexual access to his wife. 72.9 per cent women respondents replied that they have to undergo forced sex. 57.2 per cent made physical relations twice in a week. Husbands feels it birth right to have physical relations after getting marriage. He ignores wife's emotions, acceptability or even her health. This is due to the ego of Indian males, through which he used to go for forced sex by all means.
13. 13.3 per cent women respondents have hospitalized in emergency during major injury. Women whose partner abuse them physically and sexually are at a higher risk of being seriously injured and killed.
14. The abuser is always responsible for the violence, and should be held accountable. There is no excuse for domestic violence and the victim is never responsible for the abuser's behaviour. 'Blame the victim' is something that abusers will often do to make excuses for their behaviour, and quite often they manage to

convince their victims that the abuse is indeed their fault. Culture equitably values and relies on experiences and leadership from all members of society, including persons belonging to any historically oppressed group that has experienced systemic restrictions on their rights. Diverse people are engaged within their communities in activities promoting healthy relationships and healthy sexuality. Many promoting factors have been identified supporting domestic violence, 65 per cent women respondents replied that their counterparts became cruel due to provoking by their friends, 55.8 per cent respondents admits that being beautiful also creates complexes among males, due to which he suspects her and starts threatening. 32.5 per cent respondents admits the cruel behaviour arises due to extra marital relations, because husbands feels that he is not been able to do justice with his family and in overcoming this complex he starts violence.

15. Participation of women in political system, from a old time women lived in parda system in recent time women reservation bill were not passed in proper way so it is again a main cause and few women in parliament, fourth rank (1.68) to risk of challenge to religious laws. Roles of women and others and given the last rank to proprietary rights. Investigations by human rights watch have found that cases of domestic violence, law enforcement officials frequently reinforce the batterer's attempts to control and demean their victims.
16. Stress may be increased when a person is living in a family situation, with increased pressures. Social stresses, due to inadequate finances or other such problems in a family may further increase tensions. Violence is not always caused by stress, but may be one way that some people respond to stress. Families and couples in poverty may be more likely to experience

domestic violence, due to increased stress and conflicts about finances and other aspects. Some speculate that poverty may hinder a man's ability to live up to his idea of 'successful manhood', thus he fears losing honour and respect. Theory suggests that when he is unable to economically support his wife, and maintain control, he may turn to misogyny, substance abuse, and crime as ways to express masculinity. 82.5 per cent women replied that they have become aware by viewing television serials and keep an eye on their counterparts. 66.7 per cent women replied that violence is commonly seen in extra marital relations in media. Domestic violence can be prevented by sting operations.

17. 70.0 per cent women respondents accepted of being sterile women, which has given rise to arises of domestic violence whereas, 62.1 per cent respondents were faced problems due to difference of education of partner couple. 55.0 per cent respondents accept the cause of violence due to age difference of partner whereas, 51.7 per cent women accepted that their counterparts are engaged in extra marital relationship. 55.4 per cent respondents were having have difference of behaviour of the partner whereas, 47.1 per cent respondents were faced mental illness to be the cause of violence. 37.9 per cent women respondents were faced violence due to dowry in whereas, 36.7 per cent women were faced in-laws interference in personal life. 25.0 per cent women were faced causes of violence due to over confidence and 31.66 per cent due to beauty. 34.2 per cent women respondents were suffering from frustration in daily life causes violence whereas, 28.3 per cent women were replied that have lack of money causes the violence. 24.6 per cent respondents admits unemployment factor as the cause of violence.

18. The impact of violence on women's mental health leads to severe and fatal consequences. Health consequences

of violence against women in physical health outcomes are injury, unwanted pregnancy, miscarriage, pelvic inflammatory disease, chronic pelvic pain, asthma, headaches, irritable bowel syndrome and self-injurious (smoking, unprotected sex). Mental health outcomes like depression, fear, anxiety and post traumatic stress disorder and fatal outcomes like suicide, maternal mortality and HIV. Fourth rank (1.45) to impact on children who have witnessed domestic violence or have themselves been abused, exhibit health and behaviour problems. They may try to run away or even display suicidal tendencies. Battered women have tendency to remain quiet, agonized and emotionally disturbed after the occurrence of the torment. A psychological set back and trauma because of domestic violence affects women's productivity in all forms of life. The suicide case of such victimized women is also a deadly consequence and the number of such cases is increasing. A working Indian woman may drop out from work place because of the ill-treatment at home or office, she may lose her inefficiency in work. Her health may deteriorate if she is not well physically and mentally. Some women leave their home immediately after first few atrocious attacks and try to become self-dependent. Their survival becomes difficult and painful when they have to work hard for earning two meals a day. Many such women come under rescue of women welfare organizations like Women Welfare Association of India (WWAI), Affus Woman Welfare Association (AWWA) and Woman's Emancipation and Development Trust (WEDT). Some of them who leave their homes are forcefully involved in women trafficking and pornography. This results in acquiring a higher risk of becoming a drug addict and suffering from HIV/AIDS. Some of course do it by their choice.

Perhaps the most crucial consequence of violence against women and girls is the denial of fundamental human rights to women and girls. International human rights instruments such as the Universal Declaration of Human Rights (UDHR), adopted in 1948, the Convention on the Elimination of All Forms of Discrimination Against Women (CEDAW), adopted in 1979, and the Convention on the Rights of the Child (CRC), adopted in 1989, affirm the principles of fundamental rights and freedoms of every human being. Both CEDAW and the CRC are guided by a broad concept of human rights that stretches beyond civil and political rights to the core issues of economic survival, health, and education that affect the quality of daily life for most women and children. The two conventions call for the right to protection from gender-based abuse and neglect.

19. The abuser need to feel in-charge of the relationship. 24.2 per cent women were found to have in isolation in order to increase dependence on him an abusive partner will cut off from the outside world. 15.8 per cent women have put on threats to keep their victims from leaving or to scare them into dropping charges. 9.6 per cent women were used intimidation tactics designed to scare into submission, include making threatening looks or gestures, smashing things in front of destroying property, hurting or putting weapons on display. 3.7 per cent women were denial and blame their abusive and violent behaviour on a bad childhood and even on the victims of their abuse.

    A wide range of effects from domestic violence. The perpetrator's abusive behaviour can cause an array of health problems and physical injuries. Victimes may require medical attention for immediate injuries, hospitalization for severe assaults, or chronic care for debilitating health problems resulting from the perpetrator's physical attacks. The direct physical effects of domestic violence can range from minor scratches or bruises to fractured bones or sexually transmitted diseases resulting from forced sexual activity and other practices. The indirect physical effects of domestic violence can range from recurring headaches or stomachaches to severe health problems due to withheld medical attention or medications.

20. 68.3 per cent women felt to have safe in society and family to preventive measures of violence whereas, 61.3 per cent women favoured preventive factors of Indian culture. 50.8 per cent women used advice of counsellor's whereas, 48.3 per cent respondents used women rights for preventive measures of violence. 38.3 per cent women were taking advice from NGO's to prevent violence.

    Further evaluation is needed to assess the effectiveness of violence as preventive measures. Interventions with promising results include increasing education and opportunities for women and girls, improving their self-esteem and negotiating skills, and reducing gender inequities in communities.

    Preventing violence against women requires the support and contributions of many patterns; federal agencies, state and local health departments, non-profit organizations, academic institutions, international agencies, and private industry. Partners help in a variety of ways, including collecting data about violence, learning about risk factors, developing strategies for prevention, and ensuring that effective prevention approaches reach those in need.

21. Correlation coefficient between domestic violence and variables, age (0.4132*), education (0.3885*), caste (0.3661*), religion (0.4672*) and income (0.4185*) significantly correlated with domestic violence like

physical abuse, sexual abuse, emotional abuse and economic abuse. Domestic violence is an abuse of power perpetrated mainly by men against women either in a relationship. The most commonly acknowledged forms are physical and sexual violence, threats and intimidation, emotional and social abuse and finally economic deprivation.

Suggestions, Recommendation and Policy Implications

1. Within the local community, partnerships have to be developed with traditional elders, religious leaders, community-based groups, neighbourhood associations, men's groups (e.g., village farmers'' associations), local councils and village level bodies.
2. Within civil society, the range of partners include professional groups, women's and men's groups, NGOs, the private sector, the media, academia, and trade unions.
3. At the state level, strategies must be designed in partnership with the criminal justice system (the police, judiciary and lawyers); the health care system; parliament and provincial legislative bodies; and the education sector.
4. At the international level, the stakeholders include international organizations (such as the United Nations agencies, the World Bank, and the regional development banks). Domestic violence is a health, legal, economic, educational, developmental and human rights problem. Strategies should be designed to operate across a broad range of areas depending upon the context in which they are delivered. Key areas for intervention include :
    - Advocacy and awareness raising
    - Education for building a culture of non-violence

- Training
- Resource development
- Direct service provision to victim-survivors and perpetrators
- Networking and community mobilization
- Direct intervention to help victim-survivors rebuild their lives
- Legal reform
- Monitoring interventions and measures
- Data collection and analysis
- Early identification of 'at risk' families, communities, groups, and individuals.

5. These areas are not mutually exclusive; interventions may touch upon several areas of once.
6. Above all, five underlying principles should guide all strategies and interventions attempting to address domestic violence.
   - Prevention
   - Protection
   - Early intervention
   - Rebuilding the lives of victim-survivors
   - Accountability

   This section of the Digest attempts to formulate a framework for coordinated action at the policy and programme level. An effective strategy is one that is designed to be culture and region-specific, providing victim-survivors easy access to wide-ranging services, and involving the community and individual stakeholders in the design of interventions. By focussing on the stakeholders and by highlighting responsibilities of the family, the local community, the civil society, the state, and international organizations, this framework points to relevant areas of action.

7. The police are particularly well-positioned to provide assistance to victim-survivors, but very often their own prejudices, lack of training, and reluctance to intervene binder them from dealing with domestic violence. Training and sensitization of police at all levels must be instituted, and guidelines must be developed to monitor police response. Police must be held accountable for their own behaviour towards victim-survivors in order to prevent secondary victimization of women at their hands.
8. The judiciary can strongly reinforce the message that violence is a serious criminal matter for which the abuser will be held accountable. The judge sets the tone in the courtroom and makes the most critical decisions affecting the lives of the victim, perpetrator, and children, and must therefore be sensitive to the dynamics of domestic violence in order to pass equitable verdicts. Sensitization of the judiciary to gender issues is, therefore, critical and law schools should include relevant courses in their programmes.
9. Protective measures : The protection and safety of victim-survivors should be the prime focus of legal systems. It is important that protective measures are provided so that victim-survivors are not left without adequate protection, and are not re-victimized. In industrialized countries, women's shelters have provided support to victims of domestic violence since the 1970s, usually providing a 24-hour hotline, support groups for the victims, basic childcare, and social and legal services. Similar centers have been created in many developing countries since the early 1980s, mostly run by NGOs. Given that shelters are expensive, NGOs in developing countries are hard-pressed to provide

shelter for victims, and focus instead on providing legal advice and psychological and social support.

10. The healthcare system is well-placed to identify women who have been abused and refer them to other services, as the vast majority of women visit a health facility at some point in their lives – during pregnancy, for example, or to get treatment for themselves or their children. The reality, however, is that far from playing a proactive role, the health care system has usually been unresponsive to women suffering from domestic abuse. Training for healthcare providers is necessary to guide them on the early screening and identification of women who are suffering domestic violence. Such training, as far as possible, should be integrated into existing training programmes rather than be created as separate programmes. WHO has identified the following issues that need to be addressed in sensitizing healthcare providers:

    - Their possible negative feelings, including inadequacy, powerlessness and isolation, particularly in areas with few referral services;
    - Some cultural beliefs, including the idea that domestic violence is a private matter;
    - Possible misconceptions about victim-survivors, including the belief that women provoke violence;

    Training should be supplemented with protocols to guide healthcare providers to implement standards. Protocols should include procedures for documentation for legal, medical and statistical purposes; legal, ethical and privacy issues; and up-to-date information on local referral services. Protocols need to be culture-specific with special attention paid to respecting the rights of women.

11. Curricula that teach non-violence, conflict resolution, human rights and gender issues should be included in

elementary and secondary schools, universities, professional colleges, and other training settings. Violence against women can be prevented and eliminated only when the underlying causes of violence are addressed and cultural norms and attitudes are challenged. Curriculum reform that works towards eliminating the gender stereotyping in schools (teaching about women's contributions in history class, eliminating sex stereotypes in textbooks, promoting girls participation in sports) are important steps in achieving gender equality.

A more fundamental problem—that of girls enrolment in schools—has to be addressed by governments alongside curriculum reform. In South Asia, the Middle East and Africa, for example, girls enrolment in primary schools is well below that of boys, a phenomenon that perpetuates female subordination.

12. UNICEF works with different parameters to address domestic violence in many countries. Examples include, facilitating creation of Bolivia's National Plan for the Prevention of and Eradication of Violence Against Women (1994) and the adoption of Law 1674 against Family or Domestic Violence (1995), work with the National Jordanian Television to develop TV spots on violence against women; and support for the development of an active movement against gender based violence in Afghanistan and other countries in South Asia.
13. The United Nations regional campaigns, coordinated by UNIFEM, to eliminate violence against women have spurred new partnerships between a number of UN agencies (including UNICEF), governments, national and regional NGOs, and community-based groups and media organizations since 1998.
14. UNFPA supports research on the prevalence of domestic violence and has helped to create women's

health centres in areas where such violence is common. It also works in partnership with governments, NGOs and local communities to support programmes to eliminate FGM.

15. WHO is coordinating a multi-country study on women's health and domestic violence, which aims to develop methodologies to measure violence against women and its health consequences cross-culturally in six countries.
16. The Pan American Health Organization (PAHO) and the Inter-American Development Bank (IDB) are collaborating to pilot a coordinated, multi-sectoral response to violence against women in Latin America.
17. The Trust Fund in Support of Actions to Eliminate Violence against Women, established at UNIFEM in 1996 by a UN General Assembly resolution, has supported innovative projects around the world that address all forms of gender-based violence.
18. Fighting the 'Domestic Violence' Evil.
19. **Need for stringent laws** : The Government of India passed a Domestic Violence Bill, 2001, "To protect the rights of women who are victims of violence of any kind occurring within the family and to provide for matters connected therewith or incidental thereto.
20. **Role of Non-Governmental Organizations (NGOs) :** The role of non-governmental organizations in controlling the domestic violence and curbing its worse consequences is crucial. Sakshi—a violence intervention agency for women and children in Delhi works on cases of sexual assault, sexual harassment, child sexual abuse and domestic abuse and focuses on equality education for judges and implementation of the 1997 Supreme Court's sexual harassment guidelines. Women's Rights Initiative—another organization in the same city runs a legal aid cell for cases of domestic abuse and works

in collaboration with law enforcers in the area of domestic violence.

21. **Policy and Healthcare :** Police plays a major role in tackling the domestic violence cases. They need to be sensitized to treat domestic violence cases as seriously as any other crime. Special training to handle domestic violence cases should be imparted to police force. They should be provided with information regarding support network of judiciary, government agencies/ departments. Gender training should be made mandatory in the trainings of the police officers. There should be a separate wing of police dealing with women's issues, attached to all police stations and should be excluded from any other duty.

22. **Counselling for victims :** Due to the extent and prevalence of violence in relationships, counsellors and therapists should assess every client for domestic violence (both experienced and perpetrated). In addition to determining whether DV is present, counsellors and therapists should also make the distinction between situations where battering may have been a single, isolated incident or an ongoing pattern of control. The therapist must, however, consider that domestic violence may be present even when there has been only a single physical incident as emotional/verbal, economic, and sexual abuse may be more insidious.

23. Substantial knowledge regarding the legal aspects on the side of the field workers in order to give proper advice and referrals to the victims (workshops).

24. Improvement of the possibility of receiving free legal advice for victims.

25. Workshops should also teach screening methods for the detection of alcohol-related violence as well as their characteristics. They should also learn about legal

aspects which are important for the work with the victims and the batterers.

26. Promoting 'Social Intelligence' in children, not only intellectual and competitive behaviours.
27. Teaching girls and boys a flexible role (and family) allocation, in which the man does not dominate the woman.
28. Rising awareness regarding the association between alcohol and violence.
29. Rising awareness regarding the distorted pictures advertising gives alcohol and role allocation.
30. Increasing the alcohol taxes, stricter laws with regard to alcohol consumption for minors.
31. Awareness rising public campaigns with regard to women as independent members of society family violence as a public problem (stop tabooing the matter as a family matter).
32. Implementation and evaluation of effective programmes for the treatment of batterers.
33. Increasing the social resources and services for victims. Providing fast financial support/free legal aid for the victims, if required (e.g. in the case of separation).
34. Fostering the cooperation and exchange of experiences and knowledge among different services and multidisciplinary teams.
35. There is insufficient evidence to recommend for or against routine universal screening for violence against either pregnant or non-pregnant women.
36. There is insufficient evidence to recommend any of the following primary care interventions to prevent violence against pregnant or non-pregnant women, although decisions to do so may be made by the clinician and patient on other grounds.

37. Careful screening of family violence.
38. Referral to personal and vocational counselling.
39. There is insufficient evidence to recommend for or against screening men as potential perpetrators of violence against their intimate partner.

Bibliography

American Academy of Family Physicians (2008). 'Article on violence'; www.nlm.nih:gov/medilineplus/domestic violence.html.

American Medical Association (2001). "Article on Domestic Violence : An Overview" www.findcounseling.com/Journal/domestic violence.

Amnesty International (2007). Violence Against Women. A Fact Sheet. Broben Bodies, Shattered Minds : Torture and Treatment of Women. From www.amnestyusa.org/violence-agaisnt women.

Anonymous, article on "Domestic Violence and Abuse : Signs and Symptoms of Abusive Relationship"; www.helpguide.com.

Anonymous, article on, "Domestic Violence and Intimate Partner Abuse Causes, Risk Factors". www.medicinenet. com.

Barua, A. (2009). "Prevention of Violence Against Women". A Buddhist Perspective p. 10-14. http://mingbob. buddhistdoor.com/en/news/a/2477.

Conference on Women (1999). "Violence and Women". http.:// www.idrc.ca. com.

Corney, M.; Buttell, F. and Duttopn, D. (2007). "Women Who Perpetrate Intimate. A Review of the Literature with Recommended for Treatment". *Aggression and Violent Behaviour*, **12**(1) : 108-15. http:// en.wibipedia. org/wibi/domestic violence.

Desai, Dhruv (2007). "Sexual Harassment and Rape Laws in India", www.legalserviceindia.com/articles/rape_laws.htm.

Dissiz and Sahin (2008). Domestic Violence Against Women and Its Causes : An analysis from the Perspective of University Students. Vol. 6. Issue 5, p.no. 277-286. www.medwelljournals.com./fullest text.

Gattardo, C. (2009). "Domestic Violence is Not A Private Family Matter". www.opendemocracy.net./

Gretchen E. Ely (2004). "Stress, Trauma, and Crisis"; p. 223-241, http:// www.informa word.com.

Haytor, Lockie and Fraser (2007). "Domestic Violence and the State"; http://www.web.austin.law_librory/domestic.

Hoffman, P. (2004). "Psychological Abuse of Women by Spouses and Live in Lovers. Women and Therapy" p. 37-47. www.proc.aspc.ca/ncjv/emotional.pdf.

Issoac, L. Hmar (2010). "Violence Against Women. From www.manipluronline. com/violenceagainstwomenod.

Jena, C.K. (2007). "Violence Against Women : A Human Right Violation A.J.R. P - 312 – 319. http://airwebworld.com/article.

Kannabiran, K. and Menon, R. (2007). From Mathura to Manorama" Resisting Violence Against Women in Indian, New Delhi : Women Unlimited. http://www.deepdyvc.com//p/sag/book.review.

Kim Stuared (2007). "Bryony House—About Abuse"; www.bryonyhouse.ca/ aboutabuse.htm.

Lee Williams (2007). "Domestic Violence". http://www.articlesbase.com.

Lily Greenon (2004). "Violence Against Women – A Literature Review"; http://www.academon.com.

Lily. Greenon (2007). "Domestic Violence—An Overview of the Problem of Domestic Violence in India". http://www.academon.com.

Lynn Barkley Burnett (2002). "Article on Domestic Violence"; www. porosproject. org/Domestic_violence.doc.

Melind Smith and Jeanne Segal (2010). Contributed to this articles. Domestic Violence and Abuse from http://www.helpguide.org/

Miller and Burstow (2002). "Radical Feminist Therapy", www.phac-aspc.9c. com.

Misra, P. (2008). "Domestic Violence Against Women : Legal Control and Judicial Response. http://airwebworld.com/article/Index.

Moore, T.M.; Stuart, G.L.; Mechan, J.C.; Rhatigan, D.L.; Hellmuth, J.C. and Keen, S.M. (2008). "Drug Abuse and Aggression Between Intimate Partners. A meta-analytic review clin Psychol Rev 2008, **24**(2) : 247-274. www.biomedcentral.com.

Nandita Saikia (2007). "Domestic Violence Against Women and Children". www. Porosproject.org/NanditadiarrhoeaSaikia.doc.

Nerenberg, L. (2005). 'Physical Violence'; www.spvm.qc.ca.

Oshodi, J. (2010). "Violence Against Women Must Be Addressed in Nigeria—A Task for the First Lady. http://www.nigerianin inquirer.com/2010

Preeti Mishra (2006). "Domestic Violence Against Women : Legal Control & Judicial"; www.vedamsbook.com.

Quinn (2000). "Verbal/Emotional Abuse"; www.suite 101.com.

Raghuvendra Singh Raghuvanshi (2006). "Article on Violence Against Women." www.legalservices India.com.

Roberts (2000). "Rober's Queensland Study on Literature Review Family and Domesic Violence in Culturally"; http://www.communities.wa.gov. pdf.

Sharma, K. (2009). "Violence Against Women in India Has Gone Up". One World South Asia. Southasia.oneworld.net/

Sheela Saravanan (2000). "Violence Agiant Women in India—A Literature Review". http;//www.idrc.ca/uploads/user_pdf.

Shorey, R.C.; Cornelius, T.L. and Bell, K.M. (2008). Behavioural Theory and Domestic Theory : A Framework for Prevention Programming. *Journal of Behaviour Analysis of Offender and Victim : Treatment and Prevention*, **1**(4) : 1-13. http:/en.wibipedia.org/wibi/domestic violence

Singh, A.K.; Singh, S.P. and Pandey, S.P. (2009). Madhow Book "Domestic Violence Against Women in India" 442 p. ISBN, 81-907891. http://www. Vedamsbooks.in/no61541.htm.

Soli Sorabjee (2006). "Article on Domestic Violence." www.Indian Express.com.

Sreenivasulu, N.S. (2008). "Human Rights Many Sides to a Coin. p. 226-230. http://airwebworld.comarticle/Index.

The Organisation for Economic Cooperation and Development (2010). Development Centre" together with ICRW andf UNDF. hattp:www.icrw. org/whatwedo/violence against women

The Times of India (2008). "Violence Against Women". http://airwebworld.com/ article/Index.

Thompson, R.S.; Rivaro, F.P. and Thompson, D.C. (2009). Identification and Management of Domestic Violence :> a randomized trial. p. 253-263.

Thomson Gale (2005). "Domestic Violence from World of Health", www.suite 101.com.

Tjaden and Thoennes (2000). "Domestic Violence—Wikipedia the Free Encyclopedia"' http://www.wikipedia.org/wiki/Domestic_violence.

Tomita (1999). "Elder Abuse and Neglect : Causes, Diagnosis and Intervention Strategies" www. Preventelderabuse. Org./elderabuse/sdiarrhoeaabuse. html.

U.S. Department of Justice (2007). "About Domestic Violence" Rebived 24, 2010. http://en.wibipedia.org/wibi/domestic violence

U.S. Office "Domestic Violence – Wikipedia, The Free Encyclopedia". http://www. wikipedia.org/wiki/Domestic_violence.

UNIFEM'S (2009). Violence Against Women and Girls in One of the Most Widespread Violations of Human Rights From – Unifem.org/gender-issues/violence.against.women.

United Nation Study (1998). "Women : Victims of Violence"; http://www. womenaid. org/press/info/violence/victims violence. html.

Vernon J. Geberth (1998). "Practical Homicide Investigation LAW and ORDER magazine." www.serve.com/PHIHOM/articles/domviolence.htm.

Walby, S. and Myhill, D. (2008). Assessing and Managing the Risk of Domestic Violence (London – Home Office). http://mingbob. budhistdoor.com

Wechsler (2003). "Definitions of Domestic Violence"; www.combativiolence against women.org/domestic violence. html.

Williamson (2000). "Handbook for First Nations Women : Domestic Abuse, Legal Rights"; www.woman abuse prevention. Com/html/emotional_ abuse_literature_rev. htm.

Williamson (2004). "Introduction to Domestic Violence". www.ocalynchburg. com/domestic violence/introduction.htm.

Women Health Gov. (2009). "Violence Against Women". National Domestic Violence. From http://www.womenshealth.gov./violence/

Women's Service Network (2000). "Rural and Remote Domestic Violence Project", www.wesnet.org.

World Health Organisation (2007). "Multi Country Study on Women's Health and Domestic Violence Against Women. Vol. 33, issue 2 p. 73. http://www.ijcm.org.in/article.asp?

Index